Wounded Angels

Lessons of Courage
from Children in Crisis

Richard Kagan, PhD

Child & Family Press
Washington, DC

Child & Family Press is an imprint of the Child Welfare League of America. The Child Welfare League of America is the nation's oldest and largest membership-based child welfare organization. We are committed to engaging people everywhere in promoting the well-being of children, youth, and their families, and protecting every child from harm. Proceeds from the sale of this book support CWLA's programs benefiting children and families.

CHILD WELFARE LEAGUE OF AMERICA, INC.
HEADQUARTERS
440 First Street, NW, Third Floor, Washington, DC 20001-2085
www.cwla.org
E-mail: books@cwla.org

CURRENT PRINTING (last digit)
10 9 8 7 6 5 4 3 2 1

Cover and text design by Amy Alick Perich
Edited by Cathy Corder, Tegan A. Culler, and Peggy Porter Tierney

Printed in the United States of America

ISBN # 0-87868-747-5

Library of Congress Cataloging-in-Publication Data

Kagan, Richard.
  Wounded angels : lessons of courage from children in crisis / Richard
Kagan.
    p. cm.
  ISBN 0-87868-747-5
  1. Psychic trauma in children--Case studies. I. Title.
  RJ506.P66K34 2003
  618.92'852109--dc21
                          2003005170

*This book is dedicated
to Laura, my angel;
to the memory of my Grandma Eva;
and
to all the children who lit my way.*

Angels are messages from God.
They come to tell us what is important,
true, essential, and fundamental.

–Rabbi Karyn D. Kedar
God Whispers: Stories of the Soul, Lessons of the Heart

Also by Richard Kagan:

*Rebuilding Attachments with Traumatized Children:
Healing from Losses, Violence, Abuse, and Neglect*

Real Life Heroes: A Life Storybook for Children

*Turmoil to Turning Points: Building Hope for
Children in Crisis Placements*

Families in Perpetual Crisis (with Shirley Schlosberg)

CONTENTS

ACKNOWLEDGMENTS

I have been blessed with the support of my wife, our children, my parents, and my brothers, sisters, and their spouses. My wife, Laura; my children, Josh, Michael, and Michelle; and my daughter-in-law, Cindy, helped me shape this book and kept me focused on what really matters. Laura shared with me the richness of spirituality and our Jewish heritage and challenged me to regain a sense of balance in my life when I became consumed with my work. My parents and brothers helped me edit the first chapters. My daughter and sons helped me chapter by chapter to keep this book focused and readable.

Friends, colleagues, and editors enriched my writing and understanding. I am especially grateful to Ron Gerhard, Sudha Hunziker, Phil Rosenberg, and Steve Prudente for helping me to edit this book from start to finish. I would also like to thank Ray Schimmer and Natalie Nussbaum for their insights and recommendations for this book. Susan Munro, Lorraine D'Aleo, and Bonnie Unser helped me with early drafts of the first chapters. Nancy D'Amato, Christine Teiper, and Janice Houston-Little helped me with individual chapters.

Susan Brite, former Director of Publications at the Child Welfare League of America (CWLA), supported my vision for this book and made publication possible. Cathy Corder helped me with the first draft. Peggy Porter Tierney kept me from getting lost as I struggled with the rewards and frustrations of this work. She edited the first several chapters and helped me keep this book on target. I am very grateful for her diligence and critique. Tegan Culler brought this work to completion by streamlining and integrating my work and the efforts of previous editors. I am immensely grateful for how she captured the essence of this book and helped me make the stories flow without losing my voice.

This book was based on the permanency-based model of family services outlined in *Families in Perpetual Crisis* with my co-author, Shirley Schlosberg, and further developed in *Turmoil to Turning Points: Building Hope for Children in Crisis Placements.* Shirley taught me how to work with children and parents using the metaphors of unhealed wounds in family and community interventions, how pain needs to be shared, how too much pain borne by one person in a family leads to severe symptoms, and that "you can't give up what you never had." She taught me how to engage families in the midst of serial crises. I learned from her how to empower parents to take charge of their work to reunite or prevent placements and to "stop me if I ask about something too nosy." Shirley taught her staff to look at what good parents do for 2-year-olds, how to develop interventions that fit the developmental age of children and parents, and how to center family and network interventions on a child's need for permanency.

My understanding and practice approach was shaped by pioneers in child development, child welfare, and family therapy. My training in permanency work with children in residential treatment began with my former supervisors, Nadia Finkelstein and David Nevin. I had the privilege of learning directly from guest instructors at Parsons Professional Development Programs, including Guy Ausloos, Larry Brendtro, Robert Brooks, Elizabeth

Cole, Kay Donley, Eliana Gil, Ann Hartman, Cloe Madanes, Michael Nichols, Judith Landau Stanton, and Paul Steinhauer. More recently, I have learned valuable approaches and strategies for facilitating bonding and helping children with attachment disorders from Daniel Hughes and Terry Levy.

My emphasis on life story work was inspired by the use of life stories in older-child adoption by Claudia Jewett, by Richard Gardner's mutual storytelling therapy, and by the trauma therapy approach of Charles Figley. My approach to trauma was also shaped by the work of trauma therapists and researchers including Bessel van der Kolk and Francine Shapiro. Helping families to own and use words like "re-membering" and "en-couraging" and to rewrite their life stories was inspired by the narrative family therapy model developed by Michael White and David Epston and the work of Jill Freedman and Gene Combs.

I can't sufficiently express my admiration for the foster and adoptive parents who take children such as those described in this book and care for them 24 hours a day, seven days a week. From foster parents, I have learned strong lessons about perseverance, invaluable strategies to calm a child in crisis, and what it means to build love with a hurt child.

I am indebted to my colleagues at Parsons Child and Family Center, who have fostered and inspired my work for 26 years. None of the successes described in this book would have been possible without the courage and dedication of the Parsons staff. In most cases, I would not even have had the opportunity to meet with parents and children without the skill and perseverance of social workers who engaged families in the midst of crises. I would especially like to thank Ray Schimmer and Sudha

Hunziker for encouraging my writing and to express my heartfelt thanks to the program directors and supervisors at Parsons Child and Family Center who supported my work. Special thanks to Robin Sorriento, Julie Ball, Susan Wuerslin, Cindy Szypulski, Ellen Marcil, and Tom Doyle, who worked closely with me in the Prevention program; to Linda Smith, Suzanne d'Aversa, Marianne Milks-Hines, Denise Minnear, Barbara Henderer, Mike Donahue, and Lynn Huntley in Parsons Specialized and Therapeutic Foster Care Programs; and to Chris Celmer, Steve Roberts, Kathy Ryan, and Joe Benamati, who developed and managed the Healy Crisis Residence. Sue Parnes helped me with literature searches. Parsons' psychology staff, David Nevin, Natalie Nussbaum, Jennifer Louis, Julie O'Neill, and Jim Ansel, helped me cope with fiscal cutbacks and kept me up to date with new developments in assessments and therapeutic approaches.

—*Richard Kagan, PhD*
February 2003

1

ANGELS IN MY LIFE

Can't nothing heal without pain, you know.

–Toni Morrison
Beloved

*I*n the spring of 1956, my father entered a dark capsule to set off on a perilous mission. I could see him rocketing through dark tunnels and molten lava as he headed into the center of the earth to save the world. It was a dream, of course—my dream. I cried out to my father, "You'll be killed! Stay here! Stay with me!" My screams woke me up. I was 5 1/2 years old, lying on my grandmother's bed. My mother and grandmother had gone to bury my father.

I didn't know it then, but I was looking for angels. In many religions, angels act as messengers, guardians, and teachers. They warn us of impending danger, bring insight to our confusion, challenge us to make changes that will help us, and provide comfort in our darkest moments. I needed some way to make sense out of a world that had become cruel and heartless.

A year after my father's death, my mother remarried, to a widower with two children, a son my age and an older daughter. My mother's house and most of our belongings were sold. What remained was packed up in a few boxes. A few days later, my mother, little sister, and I moved to a small midwestern city where my new father had a job and a home. Along with my little sister, we became an instant family of six with two redheaded children and two brunettes. Not long afterward, two blonde babies made eight. This was long before remarriage and blended families became so prevalent. We were not exactly the Brady Bunch, but we tried. My mother's new husband adopted my sister and me. My mother adopted my new stepbrother and sister. My parents tried to keep to the norms of the times: Move on with your lives, start over, and succeed.

My new brother and I shared a room next to the basement, just a wall away from the storage area and the boxes packed with the few remnants of our family's past. We joked that the basement was haunted and ran quickly through the darkened storage area to our finished bedroom. It took my youngest sister, born of my mother and adoptive father's union, to break the spell that kept my brother and me away from those boxes. She pulled out the boxes one day and with them, we began to open up our past, to learn about what happened to my father and my adoptive brother and sister's mother, and to begin to grieve what had been locked away.

A climate of idealism pervaded the nation during this time. Family life was inviolable. Neglect and abuse were hushed up, and sexual abuse was simply not discussed. In my town, poor families lived far beyond the railroad tracks or out in the countryside. As a boy, my only experience with child welfare was attending school with an older youth, known for his size and his temper, from the local "home." The town's orphanage and youth residence were not far from where I lived, but they were tucked out of sight beyond a sign that warned others to stay away. My brother and I had explored the ghostly remnants of one of our state's mental asylums, but we never ventured near the boys' home. We perceived it—and the boys who lived there—as different and dangerous, clearly off limits to us. It came as a shock to me to learn that some parents didn't really care about their children. I learned this in my first "home visit."

I did not plan this visit, and it was one of my most embarrassing childhood moments. A friend and I were walking along a nearby lake when a boy called out to us from a small dock: "Hey, would you guys like to try out my boat?" I didn't recognize the boy, but the idea of borrowing a small boat on a hot summer's day was too enticing to resist. We joined him on the dock. My friend climbed in the boat and I followed, naive as ever, not questioning who this boy was or whether it was really his boat. As I leaned over to climb in, our new "friend" rammed me from the side and I fell headlong into the water.

This, of course, was a major insult, warranting a pummeling by the codes of 10-year-old boys. Even though the water was warm, I knew I looked like a fool. In fact, every inch of my soaking wet body knew that I *was* a fool. After pulling myself out of the water, the only thing to do was to chase him down, teach him a lesson, and try to regain my pride. He had a head start, but I kept gaining on him—perhaps periodically turning around to make faces at me slowed him down. I followed him onto a dead-end street at the fringe of our neighborhood, an area served by a different elementary school from my own. I was only a few paces behind when he grabbed his front door and ran inside. The screen door slammed in front of my face. Trained to be polite, I knocked.

"What is it!" barked a gruff voice. "Whadd'ya want?"

I couldn't see inside, so I opened the door and stepped in. Across from me in the living room sat a man, probably in his 40s, sitting on an old recliner and watching a baseball game on an old black-and-white TV. A stained and dirty T-shirt barely covered his bulging midriff, and he sported several days' growth of a scruffy beard. I was surprised that his hair was long in this era of crew cuts, straggling over his ears and down the back of his neck.

"Your son knocked me in the lake," I muttered as I checked out the ripped furniture, beer bottles, overflowing ashtrays, and dirt on the floor. I didn't know anyone who lived like this. The place stank of mold and cigarettes.

"So knock him around! Kick the shit out of him! Knock the little prick's head off, for all I care!"

My brief plea for adult intervention was over. This man obviously didn't subscribe to the lessons my teachers taught us each year about children going to the adult in charge for help in a conflict. I walked back out of the house and onto the gravel driveway. My adversary appeared outside, standing by an old, beat-up pickup truck. His eyes glared and his lips pursed. "Come on! Whatch'ya waitin' for?" he snarled, raising his fists like a boxer.

I was a couple inches taller and at least a year older, but I was a skinny kid. He was probably a better fighter. I weighed the odds, but my anger was largely gone and no one I knew was watching. It struck me that this was not my fight. "Chase me/fight me" was his game, not mine. I had been stupid enough to become a pawn in this boy's life. Sooner or later, he had to go back inside to the surly man in the recliner, the cigarette butts on the floor, and the stench. I had never seen him before and would probably never see him again.

I yelled a few of my worst curses—quite pathetic by this boy's standards, I'm sure—and left. I was ashamed still, mad at myself for being tricked. I didn't understand it then, but in one quick tumble into the lake, I had picked up the shame, fear, and rage of this boy's life. And I learned what he must have learned: "Watch your back! Never trust someone offering you anything." I had stumbled upon one of the ways that life could lead a boy to become mean.

With my tumble into the lake, I began to break out of my narrow worldview. I had discovered that just a few blocks from my suburban home was another world, far from the privileges and security I enjoyed. Later, as a teen in the 1960s, I learned that America was not the pristine land of equality and democracy that I had been taught in school to expect. But I was optimistic about my capacity to improve the world. My parents had raised us with the combined values of midwestern America and our Jewish heritage, including *Tikkun Olam*, the Jewish commandment that each person should help repair the world. My adoptive father, a chemist, worked tirelessly developing medicines to cure diseases. My mother told us that there was nothing more important in life than raising children. And before his life was cut short by an incurable disease, my father had been a sweet, gentle man who cured pain with the skills of his hands and the tools of a dentist. I would pick up his mission to save, or at least heal, a small part of the world. No simple palliatives or dogmas would suffice for me. I knew the world moved in complex ways, and I wanted to find a way to bring about genuine change.

Learning from Children and Families

I began my first full-time job in a child and family service agency at age 26. On my first day, the associate executive director came into my office, a converted playroom, and welcomed me. I was sorting through piles of papers, tossing most of them into the trash bin.

"We save paper clips here," he pointed out, and abruptly left the room.

I felt quite at home. Recycling was years away, but conservation was something I valued. In my new job, we would fight against neglect, abuse, prejudice, and the evils of the world. And we would do it with very little, even saving our paper clips. We needed everything we could get.

My primary job was to engage children and families who really didn't want to see me. Painstakingly, I planned out how I would assess family dynamics; come up with ways to help; write elegant reports; coach social workers, teachers, and child care workers on how to carry out my prescribed interventions; and move on to the next case. My other job was to train staff, both in my agency and regionally, and to rewrite the agency's philosophies and procedures manual, the core values of my agency. It was a heavy load, but I was undaunted. With my new PhD, I would chart a path toward growth and healing for children, parents, and practitioners.

It didn't go exactly as I had anticipated. I sprained my ankle in my first week of work. A 13-year-old girl narrowly missed kicking me in the groin a few weeks later. More than one social worker refused to show up for the workshops I so carefully arranged. Most of the children I saw quickly warmed up to me, but parents often ignored my "words of wisdom."

Eventually, though, it got easier. My colleagues and I worked with family members to replace risk with safety. We walked past large growling dogs, climbed broken stairs, knocked on doors, and asked where we should sit. We looked for signs of hope, helped families rebuild trust, and challenged parents to make crucial choices about caring for their children. We urged families in distress to break out of old patterns, broaden their perspectives, take risks with family loyalties and multigenerational rules, and rebuild family and cultural ties. But most of our work centered on helping parents (or, when necessary, parent substitutes) provide the bonded, nurturing relationships and safe homes their children needed.

Children in crisis are usually portrayed as horribly battered victims, dangerous predators, or defective goods damaged beyond repair. But news reports don't show the other side of the coin, the side that offers hope for change.

I have been blessed to work with children who radiated warmth and caring with each smile and embrace. I have also worked with children who slashed at their parents with butcher knives, tightened electrical cords around their own necks, and hung by their fingertips from third-floor balconies, threatening to let go. These children may seem alien, even terrifying to us. Yet we all struggle with the same basic experiences that transform our lives: births and deaths, romances and separations, successes and failures, safety and violence, attachments and losses. And children who manifest disturbing or violent behaviors are not bad, wicked, or hopelessly damaged. Their behaviors are invariably a symptom of a deeper problem a child or her family faces. These children may not be able to express to adults in words what they have experienced in their lives or what they are feeling. Instead, they act out, and their behaviors send a message, the key to what is wrong in their families, what is needed, and where to look for strength. We just need to learn how to hear and understand the child's message.

Despite all the tragedies they had experienced, the children and parents I worked with showed me that they could muster the courage to face the past and change the future. I felt emboldened by each child who dared to say out loud what he or she feared, and by parents who moved beyond the nightmare of their histories to create a different life for themselves and their children. Their courage was contagious. It challenged me to grow.

Gradually, I realized I was asking families to do what, in some ways, I had not done myself. I had learned volumes about helping others, but I kept my own hurt feelings and grief buried under my studies and my work. There is an old joke that a therapist is a person who needs therapy every day but doesn't want to pay for it. It wasn't right. I had to face my own unfinished pain and loss. Several years after earning my PhD, I set off to explore the family history that had led to my successes and my own inner turmoil. I opened myself up to the past, returning to my father's grave and visiting distant aunts and uncles to learn more about him. Then I started to learn more about my Jewish heritage, and my Grandmother Eva inspired me with stories of our family's courageous escape from pogroms and religious persecution. In her stories, I could see how I carried the drive to succeed as well as the scars of trauma. When everything in my work seemed bleak, from client traumas to funding cutbacks, the lessons I learned from my grandmother, my family, and my heritage reminded me that the wounded can struggle on and succeed.

I entered child and family services expecting to heal, but it was my work with children and families that helped me finally confront the unspoken pain I carried in my own life. Like the angels I sought as a boy to help me make sense of my grief, wounded children guided me to the path that would lead me to wholeness.

In a broader sense, each child and family I have worked with has taught me a lesson of how ordinary people can rise up to surmount tragedies. Working with them has broadened my understanding of what is possible for everyone. This is a book about what we can learn from children who act like angels, children who have moved beyond tragedies to fight for what they, their siblings, and their parents need. I would like to share the angels I have discovered, how they changed me, and how their stories* can help each of us persevere and overcome adversity. Their stories highlight the role that courage and caring can play for people of all ages and circumstances—and the rich forces in our lives that have the potential to promote healing for all of us.

---

* Each story in this book was based on the author's experiences of working with real children and families in many communities. Details and dialogues have been changed to disguise identities and protect their privacy. Dialogues were based on interviews, assessments, and interventions involving the author, but in a few instances they were developed from information presented to the author by the individuals involved or from other reports.

PART I

The Angel Inside

2

MANDY

Children long for this—a voice, a way of being heard...
If they cannot sing, they scream.

–Jonathan Kozol
Amazing Grace

Mandy sketched a picture of herself, a stocky body tilted over tiny feet like a ballerina hovering over toes too small to support her weight. Gazing sternly at her drawing, Mandy's eyes suddenly widened. She bent over her sketch, and with a few quick strokes, she added wings.

"It would be so cool," Mandy said gaily, with a soft, gentle voice. She added pictures of her mother, her younger sister, and her cousin. Like angels, they could soar to the heavens, chat with her paternal grandmother, and fly back.

I couldn't help but notice that no one in her family had a place to land, and the drawing of her mother lacked feet to stand on. Yet in her picture, Mandy could soar higher than the birds, free and easy. Mandy smiled and her eyes drifted off, a sweet child of 11 at peace in the moment.

Mandy proudly showed me a picture of angels. Like an angel, she had been sending a message again and again to everyone around her, a message of love and loyalty that warned of tragedy and pleaded for help.

Like angelic messages in religious literature, the real question was not so much the nature of Mandy's message, but whether people would listen. I have seen hundreds of girls like Mandy, often in great pain, often causing great pain. Their messages often come in disturbing packages. When family members, teachers, practitioners, and friends stop and listen to the message, wonderful things can happen: Tempers calm, children learn in school, affection grows, parents and children learn to trust each other. It's a beautiful sight. When people don't listen, it's a different story. Such children and their families become more dangerous to themselves and others. Mandy taught me once again the consequences of becoming so caught up in our beliefs about children that we don't see and don't hear what the child is showing us.

Mandy's Courage

Mandy was brought to our crisis residence with a series of reports that portrayed a juvenile delinquent and a chronic mental patient wrapped into one child. Twice in the last three months, she had been restrained and taken by ambulance to a psychiatric hospital. Mandy came with a chronology of assault, mayhem, and self-abuse—threatening her mother's boyfriend with a knife, biting herself, stabbing her arms with needles, wetting her bed, screaming out at night, provoking fights, choking a boy in her class, swearing at her teachers, assaulting her mother...the list went on and on. In the psychiatric hospital, Mandy refused her medications, punched a nurse, ran off the hospital grounds, and ended up secluded and restrained so many times that the hospital discharged her, citing no progress.

The hospital, the police, the teachers, and Marie, Mandy's mother, described a violent, out-of-control girl suffering from a disorder that imperiled her family and necessitated suspension from school. A month before I met Mandy, Marie had given birth to her boyfriend's child, an adorable baby girl. Marie was consumed with caring for her new baby, as well as her two older girls. Marie asked for help following Mandy's return from the psychiatric hospital and was offered weekend respite for Mandy, a family counselor, a parent aide, and a parent advocate. That was still not enough. On Christmas Day, Marie said she couldn't take the strain of Mandy's behavior any longer. Mandy was sent to our crisis shelter.

When I saw Mandy, she was sucking her thumb, trying to be brave in her third placement away from home. Mandy had warned the people around her of terrible things happening, and some of the worst had already occurred. I saw a girl who was still looking for help, for her mother, her sister, and now, the new baby. Maybe that's why Mandy shared her story with me. Children, like angels, keep trying to find someone who will listen.

Mandy loved her mother beyond all words, but she knew in every bone of her body that her mother needed help. It was Mandy's job to tell the landlord her mother was out when the rent was due and to walk to the corner store for her mother's cigarettes in the rain, snow, or sleet. And it was Mandy's job to grab her younger sisters, run into the bedroom, and dial 911 when her mother's boyfriends threatened her mother.

"Come here, baby," Marie would say after the police had left. Marie would hug Mandy tightly and praise her. "That guy's not gonna bother us no more."

Mandy could have been a first-class security officer. She was always on guard, ready to jump up, run for the phone, or pounce on a man who was hurting her mother. It all worked out, more or less, until Doug, her mother's new boyfriend, moved back. Mandy couldn't understand why her mother had brought him back into their apartment after kicking him out. She didn't believe a word Doug said about how he had stopped his drinking, loved them all, and was so, so very sorry about the last time he choked Marie.

"It'll never happen again," Doug swore with that solemn, puppy-dog look in his eye and his crazy half-smile.

Mandy knew better. She wasn't fooled for a minute. A few weeks later, Mandy found Doug in the kitchen sipping tequila out of a thermos. He flashed her his crooked smile, but Mandy could smell it on his breath. Her mother was still in bed. This was during the eighth month of her pregnancy and Marie was exhausted. Mandy crawled under the covers and whispered into her mother's ear, "Doug's drinking again." But Marie just sighed in that "I can't take it" tone that Mandy knew so well. She rolled over and fell back asleep.

Mandy studied the peaceful look on her mother's face. She thought to herself about the time two months earlier, when Doug had gotten drunk and held a knife to Marie's throat. A month later, he had attacked her mother again. Mandy still woke up screaming with nightmares in which she saw Doug's face, beet red and glistening with sweat, his teeth bared like an angry dog. Doug's arm muscles bulged as he pressed Mandy's mother against the wall, clenching her neck between his hands, his thumbs pressing down on her windpipe.

"You goddamn, bitch, I'm gonna break your neck!" he had roared, just inches from Marie's face, his breath stinking of beer, his teeth clenched.

Just then, he saw Mandy running toward him. She had grabbed the butcher knife from the kitchen and pointed it at his chest.

Doug threw Mandy's mother to the floor and grabbed a standing lamp, ripping the cord from the socket. "Get that bitch daughter of yours out of here! I swear I'll kill you both!"

Marie saw the wild look in her daughter's eyes. She strained to get up, fighting against the pain around her throat and the weight of Doug's baby in her belly. Six months pregnant and larger than she'd ever been, Marie felt like her own voice was choked in a vise. Doug had become like all the men she had ever known. "Call the police!" she screamed to Mandy.

Doug looked at Mandy and her mother. "You're both fuckin' bitches! Fuck you both!" Doug heaved the lamp at the wall and stomped out the door.

Marie's jaw was trembling and her eyes froze. Mandy picked up the broken lamp. She saw the fear in her mother's face and swore silently to herself that she would never let it happen again.

Two weeks later, Marie had let Doug back into the apartment. Worse, Marie had told Mandy to keep her mouth shut. Marie wanted Doug. He had a job, a good income.

"Don't you remember all the things he did for us?" Marie insisted to Mandy. "He's the best dad you've had."

That's when Mandy started getting in trouble at school—cursing teachers, smashing the globe against a brick wall, pinning a boy in her class against the floor, and screaming at Mr. Phillips, the principal. "I'm gonna kill all of you!" Mandy's shrill voice pierced the halls.

Doors opened when she screamed at school. She could see the fear in their eyes. That was good. Her fear was now their fear. The more she screamed, the angrier she got. When the police officer arrived, she was boiling. A swift kick; she knew just where to aim. Mandy heard him swear as she dove for the door. It took five of them to pin her down. Mandy was strapped in an ambulance for her first ride to the psychiatric hospital.

Hospital staff tried to calm her and teach her ways to manage her fears and her rage. But Mandy's mother only came to one family meeting, and no one looked at what was happening in her home. Mandy kept her mouth shut about the fighting at home; she would show her mother how good she could be. "I miss my Mom," she told everyone. But the day before she was supposed to go home, Mandy stabbed herself with a pencil. When the attending staff tried to take it away, she slammed the point into an aide's thigh. Mandy was locked into a room with padded walls for the night. The next day, she was sent home.

Marie gave birth and Mandy kept on getting into fights. "I'll kill you!" she screamed at Doug. "Shut up!" her mother screamed. That's when something in Mandy snapped. All she remembered was lunging at her mother, screaming at the top of her lungs, punching and kicking, tears dripping down her face.

Two police officers pulled Mandy off of her mother. She was sent again to the psychiatric hospital. This time Mandy spent most of her time in the padded room. An aide watched her through a small window. Mandy saw how everyone treated her like she was a bomb about to go off. And that's just how she felt. She would wait them out. She'd show them all how tough she could be and how stupid they all were.

After three weeks in the psychiatric hospital, Mandy was returned home and shared Thanksgiving with her family. Marie baked a pie. Doug carved the turkey, the perfect father that day, sober and kind. They talked about driving to Florida to see Marie's mother, going to the beach, a new car. Everyone smiled.

Mandy did not want to get her mother in trouble. Marie had told Mandy that what happened at home was "nobody's business." No one seemed to care, anyway. Not even the police or the hospital. Why did they take her away and let Doug stay? Why were they always demanding that she behave? "I must be really bad," Mandy thought to herself.

Two weeks after Mandy returned, Doug grabbed his baby daughter from Marie's arms. "I'm taking her away," he roared. Marie screamed. Doug spun back and glared at Marie. His right arm flew back and his hand clenched into a fist. Then he dropped the baby on the floor, right in front of Marie.

Mandy could see his face turn blood red again and smelled the beer on his breath. She hurled herself at him, but Doug knocked her off with one arm. He tore the phone out of the wall with the other. Mandy's little sister grabbed him by the leg and tried to bite him, but Doug kicked her, sending the little girl flying into the wall. By the time the police arrived, Doug had fled, leaving behind two sobbing children and a screaming baby. Marie lay crumpled on the floor.

From Tears to Hope

The hospital had diagnosed Mandy with disruptive behavior disorder and attention-deficit/hyperactivity disorder. Labels and diagnoses often miss the point. Hospitalizing Mandy missed the point, too. Her message had not been heard.

When I met Mandy, she was still looking for help. In the picture she drew for me, Mandy soared into the sky to find her father's mother, a woman who had helped hold the family together with love and strength until her death. Mandy was showing her mother, her siblings, and everyone else who cared what she and her family needed.

It was not too late to help her, her mother, her sisters, or even Doug, but I worried that the people she loved were so focused on Mandy's behaviors that they would miss their own. Mandy had taken on the danger in her family and now embodied everyone's worst fears. She could hurt herself or someone else at any moment.

I met with Marie and Mandy together and described how Mandy impressed me with her love for her mother and sisters. I shared Mandy's picture of her family as angels and told Marie how Mandy wanted to soar into the clouds with her family.

"Over and over, Mandy shared with me how much she wants to protect all of you. She's like a little guard, ready to fight off anyone who might hurt her family." Mandy looked up at her mother. "I think she's a heroine fighting for her family," I continued. "And that tells me she must have gotten love from someone."

I felt a little twinge in my stomach and hoped that Marie would not lash out in reply. After all, she probably expected to hear an assessment from me of all her daughter's problems. I looked at Marie. To my relief, I saw tears forming in her eyes. Marie looked down at her daughter. Their eyes met for an instant, but Mandy turned away. She began drawing more pictures.

"Mandy told me how much she missed you. I'm surprised she's not in your lap right now. She also shared with me some of the times she tried to stop Doug from hurting you."

Marie looked up, her mouth tightened. "I should never have let him back in," she whispered.

In that meeting, two weeks after Christmas, Marie promised she would stop the fighting, would never let Doug back, and would never let a man get between her and her children again. I asked Mandy what she would do if she thought her mother's new boyfriend was becoming dangerous. "I'd beat him up!" she replied.

It was a matter of fact. Mandy had been fighting to protect her mother since she was 3 years old. Marie shared how Mandy's father had beat her, how she left him after her third hospitalization. Mandy had grown up on guard duty, always ready to jump on and beat up anyone who threatened her family. This wasn't a medical disorder that could be treated apart from Mandy's life and the role she played in her family. Almost all her life, Mandy had saved her mother, her sister, and now her baby sister by calling the police and attacking men like Doug.

In a meeting we held later with other service providers, Marie cried again telling her story. I felt myself wanting to help her. "You know, it's the tears that give me hope," I interjected. "I can see where Mandy gets her sensitive side. I can see why she misses you so much."

In our sessions that day, Marie heard her daughter and recognized how Mandy had tried to warn her about Doug. In fact, Mandy had tried to warn everyone around her by reenacting the violence and danger in her home.

"It wasn't Mandy's fault." Marie said, looking down at her daughter. "I can't keep her safe."

I was struck by Marie's honesty. She had said out loud what Mandy already knew, a painful message but the truth about their lives. By acknowledging the reality, Marie was providing a chance for her daughter to heal.

Mandy had never stopped sending her message and never stopped loving her mother. Once she was safe enough to tell her story and to see that she was believed, she could calm down enough to play and study and learn, like any other child. But first Mandy needed to see that the people she loved had heard her message. Mandy's aggression demonstrated her pain, her vulnerability, and her rage. But she also showed enormous perseverance and strength by continuing to look for help and facing the traumas in her life head on. She did not give up, and Marie was eventually able to face the terror that had shaped her daughter's life. Although Marie could not safely take her daughter home, she gave Mandy permission to release the secrets she carried. Marie was taking back her role as the parent and guardian of her family.

"It wasn't Mandy," Marie said. "I should have done more."

I felt sad for Marie, but I was also warmed inside by her message. Marie had enabled her daughter to come down from the clouds, to land on the ground, and to let someone else watch over the family. Mandy and Marie taught me once again how crucial it was to see beyond a child's behaviors and to listen for the voice of an angel.

3

PATHWAYS TO ANGELS

*The task of listening to every voice is not
for saints alone; it is not too hard for
ordinary people, in ordinary times.*

–Vivian Paley
The Kindness of Children

A chunky 10-year-old sullenly stared at the door, ignoring me, her arms tightly crossed over her stomach. Her mouth stiffened and she thrust her jaws forward as though she was about to bite someone. Her voice rasped in a whisper, "When can I go?" She made it clear that she would rather be somewhere else— anywhere else, in fact—and was not about to do any "tests." I invited her to think about a few "pretend" questions before we finished.

"What would you do," I asked, "if one day, your grandma knocked on the door of your foster home?" The tension in her cheeks vanished like a veil lifting from her face. A smile emerged, a gentle, welcoming smile. "I'd hug her and hug her and make her coffee!" came the response. This girl's joy in the memory of her grandmother illustrated tenderness, longing, and affection—a pathway to healing.

If we can get beyond the glares and tantrums, we can track the traces of caring, longing, and hope that linger in traumatized children. I make up pretend situations and use drawings and tests to find out whom a child cares for and who cares for them. Whom do they long to see? Whom does a child look to for help? Who helped them in the past when they were hurt or sick? Who cares enough to guide and protect the child into the future? What would they do if the key people in their lives came to visit them? Would they run away, bar the door, or jump into their arms? I follow the traces of caring to find the part of the child, however deep in his or her core, that is still seeking to heal. This is the angel, the message of hope.

I make children aware that I respect their wishes to be part of their families and that I am not going to blame or attack the people they love. Instead, I look for the child's help in identifying obstacles that must be overcome for that child and other family members to strengthen love and caring in a family. I want to know dreams the child guards inside. It can be just a glimmer of a memory or a motion-picture-length fantasy. A fleeting recollection may be the best thing in a lonely child's life.

One 17-year-old dropout remembered how her great-grandmother spent hours preparing delicious Italian foods, "just for Joannie." These were magic words from Great-Grandma, the only person Joannie could remember ever showing her that she was special, that she mattered, that she deserved the best. Years later, in the worst of times, memories of those dinners and her great grandmother's voice saying "just for Joannie" helped this young woman persevere.

Even when a child has lost both her parents or lived for years surrounded by drugs and violence, an ember of hope almost always remains hidden deep inside, protected from the cruel forces in the child's life. If the child is protected, believed, and cared for, this ember can become a tiny flame and ignite the healing forces of positive change. When children's experiences, good and bad, have been validated by people they love and people with the power and determination to help them and their family, their sense of safety begins to strengthen and expand. Secrets and solutions emerge, often in a very direct plea.

"I want to go home, Mom. No more hitting," one girl in a crisis shelter pleaded.

"Take me home—just stop the sex," a boy told his father.

Our challenge is to hear the child's message and make it safe for the angel to emerge.

ALEX

History, despite its wrenching pain,
Cannot be unlived, but if faced
With courage, need not be lived again.

–Maya Angelou
"On the Pulse of Morning"

Alex sat silently with his back arched upward, staring upward into a blue sky. Without looking down, he picked up a small stone, tossed it carelessly into the air, and watched it narrowly miss his face on the way down. Next, he grabbed a small chunk of dirt and heaved it high over his head. The clump of dirt fell backward, struck the back of his head, and shattered into dust. A tiny leaf fluttered down, landing in his hair.

Seven other children climbed on monkey bars, shot baskets, and tried out the swings. But Alex sat silently, tossing dirt, twigs, and stones over his head. Faster and faster, his hands began to grab and throw. Clumps of dirt struck his head and burst open, streaking his face with layers of dust. Alex stared into space. His back was rigid and erect. His lips were pursed as the cascade of debris fell upon him. Dead leaves clung to his shirt.

A child care worker approached Alex."You can watch me cut my arm tonight," Alex hissed at her, his voice like a small, angry cat. Alex looked down. His forehead furrowed and his fingers clenched more rocks and dirt.

I met Alex the next day at our crisis residence. Teachers in Alex's public school had struggled to hold him down twice in the week preceding his placement and refused to take him back to his classroom. Two weeks before, the county's mobile crisis team had been summoned when Alex climbed up on a high windowsill, two stories above the school's gym, and refused to come down. Alex had a reputation for provoking fights with the school bullies, and several times a week, he was knocked to the ground or ended up with bruises. But this didn't stop him from threatening others with his 15-year-old cousin who he insisted would kill his enemies. Early in the school year, Alex told a classmate he was whittling spear-like weapons to get his revenge. Alex's mother complained that spanking him didn't help, and the school's social worker recommended a short respite placement away from home to cool things down, to prevent the hitting at home from escalating, and hopefully to get Alex back into his community school.

I saw Alex sitting stone-like and stiff on the far edge of a group of children engaged in a class discussion at our crisis residence. He had short black hair, a tall, lanky body, and dark skin, like coffee with a little cream. He was the only child that week of mixed racial heritage. Alex's father was white and had no contact with him. He and his mother lived alone in a neighborhood known for violence and drugs.

Of more concern, staff had seen little evidence of affection between Alex and his mother when she visited. Most young children placed away from home will run up to their parents when they visit. Alex hung back, and his mother barely smiled in greeting him. Alex had told staff that his mother sent him to the crisis residence because he was "bad." Rejected from his school, sent away from home by his mother, and cut off from his family, Alex was showing us what he thought he deserved: "Cover me with dirt and leaves," he seemed to say. "I don't merit your concern."

Alex barely spoke to staff or the other children, and I doubted he would easily warm up to me, a stranger in his life. My first thought was that he would refuse to even come with me, let alone to share anything that we might use to help him and his family. Perhaps, over the course of a few sessions, I could begin to win his confidence, but I didn't have that luxury. Time was scarce in the crisis residence, both for Alex and for me. In some ways, however, the best part of short placements is that you have to move quickly. Children can't wait weeks or months for the adults in their lives to figure out what is going wrong. The longer they wait, the more hope they lose, the more frightened they become, and the harder they work to protect themselves, usually by displaying angry, aggressive, and self-destructive behaviors. But the flip side is just as true: When we work quickly, the changes in children are almost magical. We just have to know where to focus.

Finding the Angel

At first glance, a 10-year-old boy streaked with dirt inspires little hope. But I knew that Alex's behavior was a distress signal: Showering himself with mud and dirt was Alex's way of getting help for himself and his family. He had not given up. My job was to make it safe enough for the spark of hope inside him to grow. Just as a zebra's stripes only make sense when you see a herd in motion, I would have to understand Alex in the context of his life, his family, and his community to make sense of what he was trying to tell me.

Safety for a child is finding someone who cares enough to accept the child as a whole person, good deeds and bad, love and anger, successes and failures, pride and shame—someone to trust. Alex was no different than me or anyone else. He just needed a link he could count on through thick and thin.

I asked the crisis residence social worker if Alex was close to anyone and learned that he was fond of his school social worker, Miss Johnson, a colleague I had known from years before. With great luck, we were able to get Miss Johnson on the phone.

A child care worker introduced me to Alex, and I told him I worked with the crisis residence and wanted to talk with him. He quickly pursed his lips and looked down, pretty much as I had expected. I added that Miss Johnson was on the phone, that I knew her from working in the agency, and that she would like to talk to him. Alex looked briefly into my eyes, pulled himself out of his seat, and in an instant was moving past us toward the phone. He picked up the phone and his face suddenly relaxed. You could see his cheeks begin to soften. His eyes began to shine. As he talked, a little smile emerged at the corners of his lips.

"I know Dr. Kagan. You can talk to him. He's going to help me to work with you and your mother," Miss Johnson told him over the phone. Five minutes later, Alex was sitting with me by himself and very busily drawing a picture of a 30-year-old woman cheerfully walking to her mother's house for her mother's birthday party.

I tried to trace signs of caring and love. Alex liked imagining pretend situations, and I asked him if he would take anyone with him to a magical island. "My aunt, my cousin, my three brothers, my father [Alex's stepfather], and two friends."

I was glad he had people in his life he looked to, but worried about how his mother fit in. "Would you take anyone else?" I asked.

"The poor people," Alex replied with a solemn look.

Alex spoke in a soft, staccato voice and told me how he had been born on a Caribbean island, lived with his mother and father for a year, and then with his mother and stepfather, Robbie. His mother moved to the United States when he was 5 years old, and he lived for the next two years with his stepfather and half-brother. A year ago, he had moved to the United States to join his mother.

I asked what he would do if there was a knock on the door and it was his stepfather, Robbie. Alex's face lit up. "I would hug him," he replied. Alex remembered how he used to watch his stepfather fix things around the house while his mother worked. "He's my godfather," Alex said about Robbie. "He'd watch us. Where he goes, we go."

I asked Alex what he would do if his mother came to the door. Alex said he'd let her in but would say nothing and do nothing. I asked what he would do if his birthfather came to the door, a man with whom Alex had had no contact since he was a toddler. "I'd let him in. I'd ask my mother, 'Can I spend the summer with him?' If she say yes, I pack my bags and go with him." Alex replied. Without hesitating, Alex was saying he would go off with a man who was essentially a stranger to him. I worried again about the depth of his relationship to his mother.

I showed Alex a picture of a man and a woman looking angrily at a girl standing by an unmade bed and asked him to make up a story. "Her mother about to hit her," said Alex. "The father say, 'Stop.'"

"What could help the girl and the mother?" I asked gently.

"She should just go to bed and say sorry to her mother." Alex replied.

Alex told me that his mom got married and he stayed with his aunt. Alex explained that his mother had gone back to the Caribbean for four weeks during his last summer vacation and had married his godfather. Alex also spent most weekday afternoons after school at his aunt's home. If Alex won a million dollars, he told me he'd give it all to his aunt. "She got a lot of problems. She's gonna change her baby's name," Alex added, and his face began to tighten again.

"How come?" I asked.

"Her boyfriend, he cut himself in the middle of the night." Alex stammered softly, pointing to his heart. "Then he called the police and said that my aunt did it." Alex looked up suddenly and scowled. "Her boyfriend blamed everything on her. She gave him a second chance staying with her, but he still did stuff."

I asked what happened with his aunt and her boyfriend. "Sometimes my aunt cry," Alex replied, looking down again. His lips were pursed now and his eyes had a glazed look. I knew Alex had drifted off, thinking about what happened with his aunt. Both of us sat silently. We could hear the other children walking out of the building to go outside. "Can I go?" Alex asked suddenly. His back arched and he was out of his seat. I knew he needed some time to collect himself.

We walked out to the playground area and found that the other children were seated around a picnic table listening to their teacher. Alex, however, immediately went to pick up a basketball.

"Alex, please join us at the table," Alex's teacher called out. Alex reluctantly obeyed, and I walked back into the building. This was a big mistake. Alex had thought the children were getting some free time outside. He needed a break after talking about his aunt, and instead of getting some time to unwind, I had brought him right into a group lesson.

Three minutes later, I heard Alex being escorted back into the building. He had refused to do any work with the class. Once inside, he grabbed the first objects he could get his hands on and began throwing them, first at a wall, then at a child care worker. Alex kept grabbing and throwing until two child care staff came over. Then, he began punching and kicking them as hard as he could. Five minutes after Alex had left me, I saw him being held to the floor, his arms and feet flailing, with two staff pinning him down. A loud screech echoed down the hall as Alex struggled like an animal caught in a trap. I walked over, filled with guilt for not getting him a break. "Alex," I started, but my soft words were answered by his thrashing. It was not the time to talk.

The Lioness

Alex was showing us his nightmare. He lived in a world where he felt alone and rejected. Mothers hit children. Alex had bonded to his stepfather, but moving to the United States had meant not seeing his stepfather for over a year. And now he had been sent off by his mother because he was "bad." Alex showed me that he cared about the "poor people" and worried about his aunt. Remembering the story of his aunt's boyfriend cutting his chest was enough to put Alex back into a trance-like state where nobody was safe.

I wondered who would provide Alex with the caring and safety he needed? Would he be better off with his stepfather? What was Alex trying to show us with his throwing, kicking, and hitting?

It took me a week to find a time to see Alex again and to meet Selina, his mother. To my surprise, he bounded into the office I had borrowed with a big smile. "My mom's coming!" he announced. His voice sounded like a little trumpet heralding the coming of the king. I asked Alex to draw a picture of his mother, and he drew a large figure of a woman with long flowing hair, her hands behind her back, and a smile on her face.

Selina was a tall, thin woman who looked older than her age. She smiled, and I was reminded of the woman smiling in Alex's drawing. Selina nodded to me and Alex and sat down across from her son. Her warm smile contrasted with the large growling lion on her sweater.

I welcomed Selina, introduced myself, thanked her for coming, and asked if she would talk about how life where she grew up compared with life in the United States. I told Selina I knew little about her island and wanted to learn about her culture and expectations, so I could understand better what Alex was showing us.

"My mother left me to make a life for herself," Selina began. "She sent me to live with her mother on our island. I didn't really know my father. My grandmother had her own house and a large garden. She was a very important woman." Selina continued to smile but her voice deepened and her face tightened, like Alex when he told me about his aunt. "She was not a person who showed love."

I felt my stomach tighten. Selina continued to smile. I knew what was coming next.

"It was hatred, anger, and revenge, often senseless," she said.

I have heard a thousand stories of abuse, and each one reminds me of how cruel people can be and how lucky most of us have been. I didn't want to hear another story of violence, but I knew that Selina needed to talk and Alex needed to learn why his mother acted as she did. I reminded myself that this was a woman who had survived and pulled herself together to build a better life. This was not a tragedy. Selina was a fighter. We needed to start with the reality of the past to build a better future.

Alex looked on with a sad, dreamy look as his mother went on. Alex must have sensed what was coming.

"She beat me and my older sisters until the blood came out. She used six wires at once and stones. My grandmother liked to see the blood. She'd smile when the blood came."

I had not asked about her upbringing. Maybe Selina expected that this was what you did with a psychologist. I thanked her for being so open and wondered if she knew what had happened to her grandmother that had led her to be so abusive. Telling me what had happened was a positive step, but I didn't want our session to end without helping Selina and Alex find a new way to understand what had happened and begin to make some changes.

"Her husband used to beat her before he died," Selina replied in a monotone. By the time Selina was 16, her older siblings had run away. Selina was left alone with her grandmother. She was not allowed to go out, and no one offered to help her. Selina learned to trust nobody.

At age 17, Selina's grandmother died and she inherited the house. "I fell in love that same year. I hoped he would love me," Selina said of Alex's father. "He was a handsome man." Selina sighed. "But he was no good. I left him."

"What was he like with Alex?" I asked.

"He made Alex say 'Thank you' as a 1-year-old. If he didn't, he'd smack him on the hand and take the food away. He hit Alex for climbing on the furniture or cabinets." Selina explained that she had to go to work while Alex's father drank and stayed home. Alex was left in his care much of his first year.

"Robbie, Alex's stepfather, was just the opposite. Sweet. A nice man!" I noticed Alex begin to smile a little, and I complimented Selina on her strength. She not only survived her grandmother's beatings but managed the house, raised food in the garden, sent her first husband away to protect her baby, and had come to the United States to build a new life. Despite a torturous childhood, Selina had strived for a better life.

I wanted to learn about the lion on her shirt. Was anyone in the family like the lion on her sweater? I looked at Alex, who grinned ever so slightly. "My mother's a lion," he whispered.

I thought of Alex provoking older youth and ending up ridiculed and bruised. "It's important to be able to protect yourself," I continued. "Sometimes it's hard to do this in a safe way."

"My son does not know how to do this," Selina declared, like a teacher reviewing a child's report card. "I try to teach him. I tell him I get mad at my coworkers at the factory, but I hold myself back. I also get angry at my child. It's natural to get angry with your child, but the love you have inside helps you to cover your anger. On my island, sometimes parents beat their children for three hours. It takes the spirit out of a person. A child loses his voice. Sometimes, Alex, he asks me to hit him. I slap Alex. I spank him, but I never beat him."

A little later, I asked Alex if it was okay to share with his mother some of the things he told me. Alex nodded. "Alex told me how much he cared about his aunt and about the time when his aunt's boyfriend cut himself and the blood came out."

"He didn't see that," Selina interjected. "You see, my sister came to see me at 3:00 in the morning. She was upset! But my sister did what she had to do. This man is no danger to her now."

I feared Selina was blocking any further talk of the real danger Alex had experienced in his aunt's home, but I pressed on. To stop now would convey to Selina and Alex that this was too much for any of us to talk about, and we would never get to what mattered most.

"I was struck by how sensitive Alex was to his aunt and how he cried when he heard this," I ventured. "He's a very caring boy. Do you think he understood what his aunt's boyfriend was threatening to do when he cut himself?"

Alex, with some coaxing, shared that he had seen other fights between his aunt and her boyfriend while his mother was out of the country and when he stayed at his aunt's home after school.

Selina turned to her son. "Aunt Ceci is okay. Why do you worry about her? You mind your own business. You need to do better in school." Alex pulled his shirt up over his mouth and slumped in his seat. His eyes locked on to his knees.

Selina frowned and her voice took on an edge. "My son is like the sheep. His fear keeps him back."

Looking from Selina, sitting tall and erect in her chair, to Alex, slumped and looking down, I saw that Alex had not learned how to be a lion like his mother. He had missed some critical element that had helped his mother endure, the element that gave her the courage to go on. Something had blocked Selina from passing on her skills and strength to deal with people. She could become the lion if she needed to but was able to hold back the lion inside herself when it was inappropriate. Outwardly, Selina was a successful immigrant, whereas Alex was a failure at school and in his new community. But more than that, Selina was ashamed of what she saw in her son.

Sometimes our children show us the very part of ourselves that we can stand the least. It's hard not to yell, or push the child to stop acting in a way that reminds us of ourselves at our worst. What we hate the most in our children is often the part of ourselves that is most in need of healing.

Alex had come to represent what Selina could not stand in herself. She had been the sheep at the hands of her abusive grandmother. As long as this was true, she could not get close enough to nurture him.

The Little Lamb

I asked Selina if she thought being sheepish kept Alex from being able to tell her before our session about what happened with his aunt.

Selina nodded. "It's the same with how he talks," Selina replied. "You see, he has not learned to speak proper English. He speaks the slang of our island. And here, in America, the other children make fun of him. So, instead of learning, he pulls back, like a little sheep. He doesn't know the words."

Alex had become largely mute. He sat with his mouth covered by his shirt. At school, he was a loner, isolated and vulnerable, a natural target for bullies. Every time he spoke, he reminded his peers and himself that he was different. His native language stood out in his inner-city neighborhood. Nor could he speak the English that his teachers demanded. Alex had not found a way to communicate to his peers or his teachers. Even at home, Alex could not voice what he saw or felt.

I grew up shy, often withdrawn. Maybe that's why Alex touched me so deeply. I knew the ways of the sheep, the fear of looking stupid that held me back, the tightening in my chest and the pain in my gut when I thought I would be called on to speak in class. I remembered the regrets I had as a child for lost opportunities, for passing up chances to stand out, for friendships I could have made. Holding back, staying on the sidelines was the safer course and fit my temperament. Over time, it became a habit and then an identity. To overcome my own shyness, I had to challenge the beliefs I held: "I must take on every challenge. Anything less than the best is no good. Mistakes cannot be tolerated." As irrational as these slogans may sound, they rang true deep inside me.

Later, as a psychologist, working with children like Alex, I learned another lesson. I had to break out of my shyness, not just for myself, but for my own children. As Alex was showing us, the nightmares and unresolved conflicts of parents frame the struggles and burdens of their children. Each of my children began in their early years with the same shy temperament that I had known.

"Quiet, creative, and reticent to speak," said their preschool teachers. I could overcome my fears or pass them on as hurdles for my children.

I set out to write articles, to lead seminars, and to speak at professional conferences. Step by step, I pushed myself outward. But I also knew that I had something that Alex lacked. I could make sense out of my shyness and how it fit in with heredity and with my role in my family, especially after the death of my father and my mother's remarriage. I also had the support (and prodding) of my wife, my brothers and sisters, and my parents to move on.

Alex needed the same things. He would begin to believe that his "sheepishness" could be overcome when he felt he had the support and safety he missed as a toddler and a stranger in the United States. He needed someone to care for him so much that they would help him rewrite his life story, from the "bad" boy, the lonely, hurt child of a wounded mother, to a hero for himself and his family. That would mean building on his courage and grappling with the traumas in his and his mother's lives.

I thought of Alex, the 10-year-old boy, and Alex as a baby. Learning to speak begins in a child's earliest months of life. This was the time when his father hit him for failing to say "Thank you." For Alex, speaking wrong meant getting a beating, and beatings for a baby can mean death. Alex learned to purse his lips to protect himself. But not daring to speak also meant not learning how to use language to express himself. What had probably helped Alex survive his first year with an abusive father had led years later to a severe handicap. Helping Alex would mean helping him gain a voice. And gaining a voice would require facing what the blood and beatings meant in his family.

By fighting with teachers and larger youth, Alex was replaying the violence of his mother's life. He was also looking for someone—hopefully his mother—to take his hand. Together, they could beat the demons of their past. Apart, Selina could go on in her life, working hard to succeed as an immigrant—but at a cost. She blocked out her past. She could go on with the tough exterior she presented to the world and try to leave all traces of herself, the hurt child, behind. Yet, while Selina proudly wore a lion on her shirt, Alex illuminated the other side of his mother, the frightened lamb who had been demeaned and cruelly beaten into submission by her grandmother. Alex carried with him the scars of their past, and the raw, unhealed wounds of his mother.

Alex was also showing us his own pain. Unlike his mother, Alex could not make it on his own. He needed a parent to love and care for him. Since his move to the United States, Alex's primary emotional connections had been with mother and his aunt. With his aunt's life in turmoil, Alex had become totally dependent on his mother.

Balancing the Sheep and the Lion

Fortuitously, Miss Johnson was able to join us for our next session. She had worked with the family, and both Selina and Alex had wanted her to join us. Miss Johnson remembered how Alex had been virtually mute when he first came to school. She shared how children from their neighborhood who resented new immigrants picked on children from other countries, like Alex. Immigrant children had to learn how to speak both proper English and African American street slang.

I wanted to talk about the sheepishness that Selina had identified as blocking Alex. Even with Miss Johnson in the room, he had returned to the position he had taken at the end of our last session. Alex marched dutifully into our meeting room but quickly pulled his arms within his sweatshirt and pulled the sweatshirt up over his mouth. "I have no arms and no mouth," Alex seemed to be telling all of us. On occasion, he whispered in response to a question. Yet, I noticed as we talked that Alex shook his head to indicate yes or no when he agreed or objected to something being said.

"Do you think you act sheepish sometimes?" I asked Alex.

"I was born that way," Alex replied in a very small voice from behind his sweatshirt.

Selina's forehead furrowed and her cheeks tightened as she turned abruptly to look at her son. I felt a momentary pang in my gut. How could I assume Selina could trust me enough to let down some of her guard? She could easily retort with another stinging rebuke of her son's weakness.

Selina's eyes clouded. "I was like a sheep when I lived with my grandmother," she replied. "Everyone beat me. My uncle, he ripped the cartilage in my knee. He dragged me around his house. My grandmother's friend, she beat me every night for saying my prayers wrong. And my grandmother hit me until the blood came out."

Once again, I was surprised by Selina's candor. She had volumes of traumas that tormented her. I also knew that telling one horror story after another would paralyze both of them. My job was to enable Selina to share the strength she carried with her son. I wanted to connect the hurt in each of them and help Selina see beyond the shame that Alex represented for her.

"I think Alex has both a sheep *and* a lion inside," I suggested. "I think he has a lot of rage behind the sheepishness."

I shared how Alex told me how he got angry when his teacher hugged other children. He felt left out. Alex said he asked to take a 10-minute break but somehow his teacher didn't seem to understand what he was trying to say. Instead of comforting him or giving him a short time-out, she ordered him to sit and work. Alex simmered and then began to burn inside. He needed to be hugged too much to be able to tolerate another child getting what he craved. Soon, he'd provoke another youth with cursing. A fight would ensue, and Alex would end up battered and removed from the class.

Alex acted the same way in our crisis residence. After talking about something that made him upset, like when he described his aunt's boyfriend to me, Alex would try to break something or kick the wall. The more staff tried to stop him, the harder he struggled. Child care staff had learned to hold back and give Alex a specific consequence, such as not being able to go swimming in a couple of hours. He would then gradually calm down.

Alex needed to learn how to be able to use his mouth to protect himself without getting into trouble by becoming the lion. Being like the sheep kept him from asking the important questions and learning the important things he needed to know to be strong. And if he couldn't ask the questions, then he could not learn the answers, just as he had not been able to master the slang of his inner city peers or the more formal English required in his classroom.

Healing the Wounds

Above all else, Alex needed a parent. The angel inside Alex had guided us to his mother's pain. Selina could not become a parent until she overcame the painful memories she carried inside. Miss

Johnson met with Alex and his mother for several months after his placement. Every week, she met first with Selina alone, and Selina shared more stories of the cruelty she had endured as a child. Selina later confided that she didn't like Alex. Alex reminded her of his father, and his sheepishness reminded Selina of the helplessness she felt as a child. But she chose to keep working to make a home for her son. After sharing her stories with Miss Johnson, Selina would bring Alex into their sessions.

Placement in the crisis residence marked a turning point for Alex and his mother. Selina could have retreated into her struggle to succeed as an immigrant and given up on her son, just as her own mother had sent Selina away to make a life for herself. We helped Selina hear Alex's call to be there for him and to mend her own wounds. Selina used the strength of the lion inside her to face again the horrors of her life.

As his mother became stronger, Alex began to overcome his own sheep-like qualities. He returned to his home and his school within a month of his placement in our crisis residence. He received help in developing his language skills. Within six months, Alex had learned to express himself with strength and clarity among his peers and in the classroom, and he had made a friend. Alex also developed the courage to say what he felt to his mother, and he no longer needed prescription medications to help him regulate his behavior.

After spending time with Miss Johnson, Selina could reach out and put her arm around her son. Alex nuzzled into his mother's chest like a toddler seeking a refuge. And the angel inside Alex could finally feel safe.

5

NICOLE

That which haunts us will always find a way out.
The wound will not heal unless given witness.
The shadow that follows us is the way in.

–Rumi

Twelve-year-old Nicole taught me the power of words—how a few remarks from adult authorities can make the difference between a child maintaining or losing faith.

Nicole tried to get help at age 3 and age 5 by telling teachers she had been touched on her private parts. Nothing was done. Her older sister was placed for a year in a residential treatment center for behavior problems and returned home. Nothing changed.

At age 12, Nicole told a teacher that the devil was chasing her in her bedroom every night. Within a week, she was placed in a private psychiatric hospital. Two weeks later, she was transferred to a state psychiatric hospital because her father lacked insurance. Two months later, I met her in our crisis residence. At that point, Nicole wrote out on paper what she could not tell me out loud—that every night, her father and her father's friend would come into her bedroom and have sexual relations with her. We asked child protective services (CPS) to indicate the sexual abuse and petition family court to protect Nicole.

"She's been diagnosed schizophrenic," the CPS worker replied. "How do you know this isn't a manifestation of her illness?"

Later, after we submitted several reports and arranged a follow-up conference, the CPS worker finally said to Nicole, "I'm not sure what was going on. I want you to stay here in the crisis residence, and then we'll find another program where you can stay for now."

"But do I have to go home?" Nicole begged, tears forming in her eyes.

"Not for now," her CPS worker replied as she got up to leave. "That's all I can say."

Tears streamed down Nicole's cheeks. She stood up and walked quickly toward her CPS worker, reaching out for a brief hug, as her worker headed for the door.

For now rang in my head. I felt sick to my stomach. It would take months to undo the harm of these words. Nicole was only 12 and well behind her grade level in understanding and reasoning ability, but she understood what "for now" meant. She could go into a group care facility "for now" and then be returned to her father. Just like her sister. Nowhere was safe.

Though her parents had refused all services, the CPS worker wouldn't believe Nicole's allegations of abuse were anything other than a product of the mental illness she had been diagnosed with. Nicole could tell us now that the "devil" was really her father. But her ticket out of her home, talking about seeing a devil at the foot of her bed, cost her support from the very authorities mandated to protect her. Also, Nicole's CPS worker didn't think she could win a case in court. The presiding judge was known to doubt children's accounts of sexual abuse, and Nicole was not a good witness: She was unpredictable, her behavior was like a much younger child, and she was not able to pinpoint details of specific dates and times when she was abused.

Nicole's nightmare was very real. CPS must make decisions based on winning court cases, but the most severely damaged children are typically the worst witnesses—and thus the least likely to be protected by the authorities that are mandated to keep them safe.

It took several months of phone calls, letters, reports, and meetings, but finally, CPS staff and the county lawyer joined us in validating Nicole. She was able to move into a foster family and gradually regained her voice. Within two years, Nicole had made it to the honor roll in her new school.

Children usually long to go home and be loved by their parents, but they also need to hear that the people who have power over their lives acknowledge their fears. For the child who continues to fear Dad's beatings or Mom's drinking, official goals to "return home" represent a message of doom unless the child hears how their parents and other important people will change. Children listen very carefully to what adults say, and especially to the official goals for their care. When their needs and wishes are recognized, they calm down. When they feel unheard, children become more depressed or agitated.

Too often, admission to mental health and juvenile justice programs has come at the expense of ignoring the neglect or abuse that led to behavior problems. Authorities often limit funding for assessments to brief diagnostic evaluations focused on justifying services, but labels such as "juvenile delinquent" or "borderline" can mask children's psychological wounds. If, as parents or professionals, we only stick to the jargon, we miss the reality behind the behavior.

JAKE

Children...are vessels of the spirit, but the spirit sometimes is
entombed; it can't get out, and so they smash it!

–Jonathan Kozol
Amazing Grace

Jake Jr. jumped to his feet, shot a quick glance at his mother
and 16-year-old sister, Becky, then turned toward me. He put his
hands on his hips and his eyes widened.

"Talk about my dad, I'll go nuts!"

Jake's voice was hard, but I also heard a quiver, a hesitation, as
if he were waiting for something, not quite sure what to do. His
words sounded like a threat, the stone-faced outlaw at high noon
ready for the gunfight. But he didn't yell, and his eyes widened.
His mother, Judy, smiled, turned her head to the side, and looked
up at the ceiling. Becky glared back silently at Jake and stroked
their baby brother, Benny. Benny squirmed in her arms trying to
get a better look at Jake.

I could see that Judy, Becky, and Benny had seen this show before. It was a repeat performance, but captivating enough to command their attention. Jake had once again taken center stage, and he had a well-documented record of scaring authorities. I supposed that I was today's guest actor, the only one without a script. That's part of the intrigue in working with families. As the "guest actor," no one could be sure what I would do. That little mystery, even by itself, can raise a sense of hope in an otherwise bleak situation.

Jake stood stiffly and didn't budge, as though his feet were locked to the floor. He had raised the flag, sounded the alarm, and stood ready to protect and defend his family against any invaders. Jake challenged everyone in the room to back away or face his wrath. A warning to all: Discuss the past and I will blow.

But in Jake's hesitation, I knew we had struck gold. Jake the Messenger was pointing the way to his family's pain, the wounds that needed to heal. The challenge was how to deal with Jake's and his family's fears in a way that would allow everyone in the family to maintain their pride.

Show and Tell

Built like a linebacker, 12-year-old Jake was often taken seriously when he roared. After threatening to break his teacher's leg, pushing and shoving peers, Jake had already earned a solid reputation as a problem kid. School was difficult, and tutoring didn't seem to help. Jake was often frustrated. Frustration led to defiance. Defiance meant trips to the principal. But nothing really changed. Then, Jake brought a gun to school. A pellet gun, actually, but a weapon nonetheless. He had enacted America's nightmare. Would Jake become the next schoolyard killer?

Jake had been automatically expelled for bringing the gun to school, but that was just the beginning. A tutor was sent to his home. "I hate her!" Jake told me when I met with him alone, a week before our family session. He smiled and chatted casually, boasting about how he pretended no one was home when the tutor rang the bell. Jake grinned. He was the hero in his battle against the tutor.

"I'd watch her through the window. She'd yell, 'Anybody home?' She'd leave after a few minutes." Jake snickered and his grin became even larger. He had defeated another teacher. Jake's smile conveyed a contagious boast that any boy who was tired of teachers' instructions and homework could admire.

After Jake's school complained to CPS, Judy began to watch for the teacher and promised to come to the door when the teacher knocked. "I blocked my mom from getting to the door!" Jake bragged. But eventually, the tutor got in. "I shot her with my squirt gun!" Jake beamed as he finished his story.

A few days later, Jake's mother received a notice that home tutoring had been canceled. Jake thought he was free of school. But then a child protective worker visited their home and urged his mother to put Jake in the crisis residence. Jake's school had insisted that he needed placement outside his home and demanded an evaluation to determine how dangerous he was. That would be my job.

I was glad to hear that he had only "fired" a squirt gun. Jake was still a little boy inside, and he had not threatened to kill anyone. But I was concerned to hear how much he loved guns. Worse, his mother had bought him the gun that he brought to school.

"Why did you bring the gun to school?" I asked Jake.

"I wanted to show it to a girl," Jake responded.

"How come?"

"Because I liked her," Jake replied in a quiet, matter-of-fact voice. He could have been reciting his current favorite TV shows. It was simply the thing to do.

Going Nuts

Jake had a 15-year-old brother, Peter, who was in plenty of trouble himself. Both boys acted like outcasts in a school that seemed to have little place for light-skinned young men of mixed race like them. The school district had filed a PINS (Person in Need of Supervision) petition on Peter, citing his chronic truancy. A few more absences, his probation officer had warned, and he would be placed in an institution for juvenile offenders.

At home, the two brothers staged a nightly drama highlighted by their fights. Peter would spot Jake throwing down his books, a game cartridge, or a gum wrapper in the wrong place in their bedroom. "I'm sick and tired of your shit on my side of the room!" he'd shout.

"Get the fuck out of here!" Jake would retort. Smaller than his brother, he had to swear louder.

"What did you say, asshole?" Peter would snarl.

"You heard, me, motherfucker!"

In a flash, Peter would pounce on his brother. "I'll kill you!" Peter would hiss, his hand around Jake's throat.

Jake would fight back as hard as he could. Sometimes he'd knock Peter into the bedpost or bruise Peter on his leg with a sharp kick. Peter would kick him in the groin. Jake would shriek, his face tightened in agony and rage. That's when Jake, younger by three years, would become what they both feared. Peter would shove Jake against the wall and dart down the street to his friend's house with Jake chasing close behind. That was the climax. Peter escaped, but Jake owned the house. He had gone "nuts."

The Weight of Violence

"Going nuts" was part of the family's dark secrets, the forces no one talked about but that continued to shape what everyone could do and say. I learned from a CPS report that Jake's father, paternal uncles, and paternal grandfather were well known in their hometown for drinking and fighting. One note mentioned that Becky had told her teacher that her father and uncle had sexually abused her, apparently while they were drinking. Another note indicated that the children's father physically abused Judy and the children.

When Becky told her teacher what her father and uncle did to her, CPS talked with Becky and her mother. But Judy, the children's mother, did not stop Jake's father from seeing the children. She did only what she had to do to comply with orders enforced by authorities. She didn't talk about what the children's father did to her, what happened to Becky, or how her sons could deal with their father's violence.

CPS staff worried about Judy and the children's safety, but they didn't have the time or training to help Peter and Jake deal with what had happened. Instead of pursuing criminal charges against the children's father for beating Judy or sexually abusing

Becky, authorities arranged for Judy and the children to move to a shelter for battered women a hundred miles away. The bus tickets they bought to send the family to another city allowed Judy to pretend that the abuse could all remain a big secret. She and the children would just start over, like magic, in a new city.

Jake learned that a man didn't have to take responsibility for what happened when he went too far. Nothing happened to his father or grandfather. The only ones who seemed to have been punished for their violence were the victims; Jake, his siblings, and his mother lost their home and the few friends they had.

Worse, the family had become further estranged from Judy's parents. Judy and her children were now living a hundred miles from her parents and brothers. A year later, her oldest brother died in a motorcycle accident. Her parents separated, and her mother became involved with a new boyfriend. For some time, Judy still talked to her father every week or so, and he sent her money. But that stopped a year later, when Judy's younger brother was convicted of murdering a man who had become involved with his girlfriend. "Grandpa's trying to help my uncle," Jake told me. "Uncle Bob didn't mean to kill the man; it just happened." Uncle Bob was another lesson about men in the family turning to violence as an answer. Uncle Bob's arrest also marked another loss for the family: Caught up in his son's legal battle, Grandpa stopped writing and sending checks to Judy and the children.

Moving to another county also meant losing contact with the child protective workers who had witnessed the effects on the children of their father's abuse and their mother's lack of action. New workers saw a family trying to make a fresh start and a mother who gladly accepted financial and concrete assistance, but balked at working to help her children overcome the abuse.

Judy initially welcomed a series of home-based family therapists, but each eventually gave up when Judy kept missing appointments—or simply didn't answer the door. Judy welcomed money for expenses and a professional "friend" to visit her every week, but Judy looked away whenever past or present problems were mentioned, and the children, watching their mother, refused to talk about what had happened.

I asked Judy who she could count on to listen to her and help her. "Nobody," Judy replied. After four years of services, Judy had neither a friend nor any family members left to turn to, no one even to call. At every point in the family saga, Jake, his mother, and siblings experienced another cutoff. With each new loss, they became more and more vulnerable.

In our session, I asked Jake who kept the family safe. He looked at Cindy, his CPS worker. "She does," he replied.

Cindy jerked back in her chair. She had thought that Judy was doing reasonably well in meeting her children's minimum requirements. Cindy only stopped by for a quick visit every two weeks. She had so many families with children who had seemed to be at far greater risk. After four years of CPS involvement, Cindy thought the basic issues of neglect and lack of protection had been resolved. Jake, however, knew otherwise.

Four years of weekly visits by a family support worker had helped Judy to get basic household furnishings, obtain financial assistance, and carry out the day-to-day shopping, cooking, and cleaning, but the core problems remained. Judy still stopped talking and turned her head away at the slightest mention of the children's father. She had never helped the children overcome what had happened when they lived with their father. She was not able to show her daughter and sons how a man and a woman could live together without fighting, and she'd never learned how to keep Peter and Jake from hurting each other.

Countdown

At age 11, Jake found himself very much alone. With the birth of his brother, Benny, Jake was suddenly displaced as the baby of the family. Now his mother spent all of her time holding, feeding, and changing Benny. No longer could Jake come into her bed late at night as her outstretched arms comforted him and pulled him away from his nightmares. Suddenly, Jake was in the same position as his older brother, Peter. Neither felt wanted anymore. Their nightly brawls grew in intensity.

More and more, Jake saw that adults and peers in his life, from his teachers to his mother, couldn't give him what he needed. His relationship with his brother was violent, and his sister ignored him. He had no real friends at school or in his neighborhood. Worse, every time he looked into the mirror, Jake knew that he was looking more and more like his father.

The number of people who cared for Jake was shrinking. "Five. Four. Three. Two. One…" It was like a countdown for a rocket about to blast off. Only instead of a rocket blasting into space, Jake had the potential to unleash a different kind of explosive force, one fueled by the secrets in his life and the fury he held inside.

Adults without close relationships become severely depressed. Children become agitated, aggressive, or withdrawn. Growth and development slows to a halt. None of us do well totally on our own, and youth and families tend to plunge into crisis as the number of true connections shrinks to one or two. When the count reaches zero, it is usually only a matter of months—if not days—before a child, a teenager, or an adult hurts themselves or someone else. As I looked at Jake, I knew that "someone else" now included our staff, the children in the crisis residence, and myself.

The Hero

Jake represented a dangerous, volatile kid to most adults. I was looking beyond the fighter for an angel. I tried to discern signs of whether Jake cared about anyone or anything. The most frightening children (and adults) I have met have stopped feeling and caring for anyone. Their hurt is so deep that they have developed a thick shell to protect them from being betrayed, abandoned, or rejected once again.

I showed Jake a picture of a man visibly arguing with a woman while a baby cried in his playpen and a little boy watched from around a corner. I wondered how Jake would see this story working out.

"The baby's crying." Jake began. "A spaceship came with aliens, big ones! They took the parents away and killed the baby. Zapped him with their lasers. The little boy ran out of the room. The aliens couldn't catch him. He jumped out the window, got to his bike, and tore off down the street. Then he found some bombs, got back on his bike. The bombs blew up the house."

"What happened to the parents?" I asked.

"The bombs killed the aliens. Then the parents escaped." Jake's eyes wandered around the room, everywhere but toward me.

"What happened at the end?"

Jake looked up, a quick glance in my direction, then his eyes moved slowly left, then right, scanning the room like searchlights searching for something, anything. "The parents didn't fight anymore. They got a new baby."

"What about the boy?" I wondered aloud, caught up in the drama. "Did he survive?"

"The boy was a hero. Can I go now?" Jake asked abruptly.

I thanked him for his stories, asked him to make up a few more, and let him rejoin the other children. Jake gave me a quick smile at the door and headed for his class.

Jake wanted to be a hero, not a killer, but he had the potential to be either. At this point, Jake was only threatening, not acting violently—a tribute to the caring he had received from his mother and others. For Jake to be a hero, he would have to learn not only to stop scaring people, but how to become a winner. He needed to develop some basic social skills—how to talk to peers, how to succeed in his schoolwork, how to win praise from a teacher, how to handle criticism, and how to calm himself down when he felt his temper rising.

Like the little boy in his story of aliens, Jake could not understand what had happened in his family. The sexual abuse of Becky reflected a lack of protection and a breakdown in trust. Becky, Peter, and Jake needed to trust their father. Instead, they had learned to live with threats and lies.

To heal from sexual abuse, children must first be provided with protection from their abusers, validation of what happened from important adults in their lives, and safety. Jake needed a parent who could face the buried trauma that Jake threatened would make him "go nuts," and the family needed to be strengthened with connections to caring adults who would watch over the children.

As Bob Dylan wrote, "When you ain't got nothin', you got nothin' to lose." The foundation of Jake's violence and anger was a series of losses. He had lost ties to his father, his paternal grand-father, and his father's relatives after the sexual abuse was disclosed, and very naturally, he missed them. Jake then lost the peers and adults in his neighborhood when the family left their community. The family could not afford bus tickets or long distance phone calls, and moving a hundred miles away severely weakened the already frayed ties to Jake's mother's family.

Although Becky had gotten some counseling for herself, Jake's mother refused to speak of what the children's father had done. It was still a mystery to the boys, a legacy of shame. Jake and Peter were left with the family's scorn and fear of their father's, uncles', and paternal grandfather's violence. As they grew into young men with sexual feelings, they silently questioned what this legacy meant for them. It was not so much that Jake and Peter did not know the gist of what happened. It was more that neither boy knew how to survive what their father did.

Time went on, but Jake remained like the 4-year-old he was when his father broke the family's trust. Inside, Jake was still a scared, needy boy. Jake wasn't out for vengeance. He was looking for someone to take control and keep everyone safe, safe from themselves and the nightmare his family members carried with them.

Counting Up, Instead of Down

When Jake threatened to "go nuts" in our family session—and hesitated—he challenged his mother, his older sister, his child protective worker, the crisis residence staff, and me to face what he believed no one could handle. This meant showing Jake that people who cared and people with power in his life could face what his father, his namesake, had done.

Later in our family session, I looked at Judy and asked her permission to talk about what happened. Judy nodded but looked away. Jake stood up.

"If you need to leave, you can take a break and then come back," I told him. Then I asked Judy's permission again, repeating my earlier message that I was counting on her to stop us if we talked about things that were too "scary."

Judy said "okay," but looked up at the ceiling. Becky, however, looked at me. I asked Becky what she remembered. She looked at her mother, then started to talk.

Perhaps out of confusion that someone dared to get past his threat, and perhaps out of his own desire to learn what happened, Jake stood frozen for a few moments and then quietly sat down. I was surprised, but relieved. This was another sign that Jake wanted help for his family and himself.

As painful as it was, Becky shared how her father and uncle had molested her and threatened to hurt her if she talked to anyone about what happened. I learned that her paternal grandfather had also molested her at another time. Her father ordered her to keep it all a secret.

I was struck by Becky's courage to speak up and complimented her. She had defied the threats; this was a tribute to her own strength. I also complimented Judy for raising such a strong daughter who must have gotten this strength from people who loved her. Becky looked at her mother. Unfortunately, I was unable to get Judy to do much more than nod and could not engage her in this meeting to show or say what she would do for her children. Despite Becky's strength, a huge gap remained in the family.

Jake stood up again a few minutes later. "Would you like to leave the room?" I asked.

"Yeah," Jake whispered. He scampered to the door, looking over his shoulder. But 10 minutes later, he came back to join us.

I felt a small stirring of hope. Jake had provided a beacon to the nightmare driving his actions, the nightmare of his family. It was just a beginning, but when you are working from zero, moving up even a small notch can mean the difference between a boy hurting someone and a boy who begins to change.

Jake could be a hero. He just needed someone with the power, the love, and the commitment to help him learn how.

Rewriting, Re-Rooting

In family therapy, we talk about the roots of a tree spreading beneath the soil. The strength of the tree depends on its roots. For a family, the roots are the connections with people who care enough to help a child and a parent deal with the reality of their lives. Roots also link each family member to their family's history of struggles, triumphs, and lessons passed on from generation to generation. A family's roots also bring in the richness of their cultural heritage and community.

Jake's case highlighted for me the dangers of severing ties to family, friends, and community. The family got help on the surface, but their remaining roots withered away. Jake still had his mother, brother, and sister, yet their relationships became more and more strained with the constraint of never talking about the past. Jake learned that his mother and relatives, the primary adults in his life, would not take charge. Without strong committed adults, the "countdown" accelerated and the secret of violence gained power. "Going nuts" became a force that that no one seemed to be able to master.

In Jake's story, aliens descended to terrorize the family. Only the little boy had the power to use bombs to get rid of the aliens and bring back his parents. Rewriting Jake's story meant enabling a parent or another adult to take over the responsibility of driving away the alien monsters and protecting the family. Only then could Jake go back to being a boy and learn ways to succeed without guns or bombs. Jake's threat of "going nuts" had not stopped me from asking about the past, or his sister Becky from discussing it. By doing so, we had helped Jake to give control back to the adults in his life. Jake finally learned he did not have to guard the secret of what his father had done any longer.

After our brief sessions, Jake calmed down his out-of-control behaviors in the crisis residence, and returned to his home. We encouraged the family's child protective worker to arrange an evaluation of Judy's ability to parent and provide a supervised living situation if she could not manage the home. We also linked Jake and his family with a day treatment program that could provide family therapy, including help for all family members to deal with the sexual abuse and to work on rebuilding Jake's connection with his mother. A special mentor was recommended for Jake, who needed to find a way to belong and to succeed with support from people who cared at home and in school.

Listening Through the Nightmare

By listening to Jake's message, we had helped Jake and his family begin to grapple with what his father had done, and by doing so, to begin to repair the tears in their own relationships as brothers and sister, mother and children. With Judy's tacit approval and Becky's courage to speak out, we had taken some of the power away from "going nuts."

Nightmares like "going nuts" have a way of following a family, no matter how far they run away. The harder we try to stifle the words, the images, and the sounds of the past, the stronger they become, until they engulf our lives with the power of what can't be forgotten. It takes strength and resolve to face our nightmares, but it's the only way healing can begin. In the same way, children like Jake can teach us what leads to threats and violence, but we have to have the courage to listen. The first step is to calm our own fears. Then we can open our eyes and ears to see and to hear what these children—our children—are teaching us.

Donald

Listen also for what goes unsaid,
and you will hear the simple truth.

—Traditional saying

*E*ight-year-old Donald tripped a boy in his class. "It was an accident," he claimed. Donald was sent once again to the principal's office. Tanya, his mother, arrived an hour later.

Tanya entered the principal's office complaining about being called so many times at work. She could lose her job. "Why can't you handle this?" she barked at the principal.

Tanya turned and scowled at her son. "Look at me when I speak!" she demanded. Donald snickered under his breath and looked down.

Tanya's hand went back. She pulled out a small stick from her coat pocket and struck him hard on his back, three times. Donald could feel the stick dig into his skin through his shirt. His eyes smarted. His back stung. Tears formed on his face.

Donald saw the principal and a teacher watching him get beaten. His whole head began to burn.

"What did the principal do?" I asked Donald as he told me this story.

"Nothing. She just watched," Donald replied. A cold look came over his eyes. In his mind, the principal had endorsed his mother's whippings.

Donald had learned an important lesson: He was on his own. Even the principal, the supreme power of the school, didn't seem to care. She did nothing to prevent or stop the beating. If Tanya had struck the principal, assault charges would have been filed. CPS was involved with the family, but Tanya left no marks on Donald, and thus, the incident did not qualify as abuse. Donald experienced how children are often treated as second-class citizens and left unprotected.

After that, Donald changed. Talking out of turn, teasing, and poking other children became knocking over desks, throwing rocks at girls, and spitting at his teacher. Donald was suspended. His mother asked the judge to place him in a treatment center as a PINS. By definition, such a statement would appear to represent Tanya's admission that she could not provide the supervision and care her son needed. In court, however, Donald was held solely responsible for his actions. To Donald, nobody in the world cared, and so neither did he. Children have often shared with me how betrayed they felt when parents and other adults in their lives watched but did nothing. From the perspective of children, neighbors and other adults condoned abuse when they pretended they didn't see or hear the violence destroying families.

Austria, Denmark, Finland, Norway, and Sweden have banned corporal punishment of children. In the United States and most countries, however, parents are permitted, and sometimes encouraged or expected, to intentionally cause pain, the definition of corporal punishment. Parents often feel pressured by relatives or neighbors to "teach a child a lesson" when a child misbehaves.

I have seen spanking work with children, but in just the opposite way that most parents wanted. Instead of teaching self-control, children learned to obey their parents temporarily, when they were being watched. They began to rely on an adult's power and threats to control their behavior. Children raised with corporal punishment, cursing, and a lack of nurturing learn to use violence as the primary solution to problems. Whippings and beatings teach children that extreme anger justifies violent revenge. That would be a great risk anywhere, but in a country with easy access to guns, it is a prescription for disaster.

I have often been impressed with how neglected children still succeeded when their talents and skills were recognized and fostered by caring teachers, coaches, relatives, or community leaders. But children like Donald, who fail in their schools and communities as well as their homes, often tap into a power they know all too well: the force of threats and violence. Children who grow up believing that they have no prospect of succeeding in the "mainstream" world can still gain power by becoming everything their neighbors fear.

I become especially frustrated when biblical phrases such as "an eye for an eye" have been used to justify corporal punishment. "An eye for an eye" represented the ancient Jewish practice of calling for just compensation for the loss incurred by another (the worth of an eye for the worth of an eye), and was never meant to be taken literally as calling for the poking out of eyes.*

This is not to imply that children whose behaviors are dangerous to themselves or others bear no responsibility for their actions. Troubled and troubling children must be challenged to grow, to look past their own self-focused needs, to learn to help others, and to make a meaningful form of restitution for any harm they have caused. In biblical times, atonement for an offense was expected to include an admission of responsibility and an apology before the community, full restitution for the worth of the damage or loss, and an extra penance defined in the Bible as 20% of the value of the offense. I have often wished we could apply this approach with youth like Donald, instead of the more typical punishments of court-ordered placements for 12 to 18 months, separating a youth from his or her community without mandating any form of apology or restitution for a youth's offenses.

---

* For a discussion of Jewish approaches to atonement, restitution, and punishment, please see Kushner, L. (1990), *The River of Light,* and (1994), *God was in this Place and I Did Not Know,* Woodstock, VT: Jewish Lights Publications. Thanks to Rabbi Scott Shpeen for reviewing the references to a Jewish perspective on "an eye for an eye."

JANINE

He who acts wild, careless is like a man without relatives.

—Navaho adage

*T*all, slim, with short-cropped hair, Janine's eyes darted right, left, and then focused straight on me. "Why do I have to see you?" A good question. As best as I could determine, Janine had seen, and been seen by, adults with fancy-sounding names and titles, running the places she found herself living in, for more than three years. Three years—ever since her mother took off one night and a neighbor heard 9-year-old Janine and her siblings screaming and fighting with each other over the last hot dog in the refrigerator.

No one had stopped Janine's nightmare. Why *should* she talk to me? Was this just another waste of time, some kind of pretend therapy?

I asked Janine to draw a picture of a person and was pleased when she picked up the paper. "I don't want markers," she objected.

Janine stared at her paper. "Why do I have to see you?" she repeated.

Obviously, my answer had not passed even the opening test. "I'd like to learn about how you see things and use that to help the people around you help you and your family," I answered. This sounded pretty weak to me. After all, Janine had just been kicked out of a group home. "Assaulted a nun" had apparently been the last straw in a long line of behavioral problems during Janine's time with that agency. "She provokes fights with other kids and runs away whenever she can. Only a miracle saved her from being hit by a truck the last time she took off," said a staff member. "We can't keep her *or* the other children safe with her here. She has to go."

Two staff from Janine's group home escorted her to the crisis residence. To some, Janine was one more victim of the drug wars in her city, an orphan of the 1990s, cut off from her parents, her siblings, and previous foster parents, and now evicted from her group home. To others, she was a time bomb, hitting and kicking at age 12. Statistically, she was at high risk for early pregnancy, drug use, and incarceration in a few short years.

I felt a weight on my shoulders, a strain in my smile. One of our first challenges in the crisis residence would be to bring together people to help Janine. People who could stick with her. People who could do more than me. With the scarce funding and fiscal cutbacks for the crisis residence, I was allotted just a few hours to work with Janine, our social work and child care staff, her siblings, her county worker, and other therapists during her short stay in the crisis residence. A few hours to come up with something that could really help her. If not, the answer to Janine's question, "Why should I see you?" would be just what she had come to expect: "No reason, it's just a waste of time."

Who would I find to help this girl? The family court judge had just terminated Janine's mother's rights after her mother once again failed to show up for court. After three years of missing visits, refusing to go for alcohol and drug treatment, and failing to provide a home, and five years of family support services, the county workers had long since given up on Janine's mother. Now the judge had finished trying.

To my surprise, Janine began sketching very slowly, with exquisite care for detail and form. Gradually, the outline of a girl's head emerged. Long, flowing hair silhouetted a Madonna-like face, a marked contrast to Janine's lean face, but the eyes were the same—strong and intense, looking straight ahead.

Janine sketched a body, glared at the paper, and sketched it again. Over and over, she traced the outline of a body, then rubbed it out with her eraser. Her mouth tensed and her back stiffened.

"Body anxiety," I remembered from my training on children's drawings. She had most likely experienced intense physical harm to herself, her siblings, or her mother. A person's body was simply not safe in Janine's world.

I hoped Janine would finish her drawing quickly so we could get on with the evaluation. Instead, she focused on every line. The head gained shoulders and part of a chest. Arms rigidly descended down to the base of the page. Janine held the paper up in front of her eyes and stared at it.

"Not right," Janine said with a soft but stern voice. Out came the eraser. The drawing went on.

Suddenly, Janine lifted her head. "I'll just draw a head," she declared in a tone that invited no challenge. The first sheet of paper was soon reduced to a crumpled ball and dropped carelessly by her side. This was a girl who found answers and moved on, a good sign.

Softly, matching the level of my voice to hers, I asked Janine some "pretend questions" while she worked. I knew Janine was not going to put up with anything resembling a standard assessment. I had to go with her pace and learn from whatever she shared. I figured I'd be lucky to get half an hour with her. A drawing, maybe two. I needed to focus on what was most important. For me, that meant who cared, who might care, and whom she cared about. I wanted to track any signs of fondness or affection, real or imagined, for family members, relatives, past foster parents, clergy—anyone who she would like to see, anyone who could offer hope of caring, comfort, and support.

I asked about aunts and uncles, grandparents and cousins. Janine looked up for a second. She said she'd like to see her Aunt Rose again but didn't know where she was.

"What would you do if there was a knock on the door and it was your brother?" I asked, hoping that asking her about her brother would open up at least a little dialogue. "I'd ask him what he was doin' here," Janine replied, without looking up from her drawing.

"What would you do with him?" I continued.

"I'd give him a big hug."

"What would you do if there was a different knock on the door and this time it was your mother?"

Janine's eyes broadened, her back straightened, and she smiled for the first time in our meeting—a broad smile that lit up the room. "I'd run and hug her."

Some would take this as a bad sign. Janine was fiercely loyal to her mother and still fighting to get her back, almost certainly a lost cause based on her mother's continued addiction and neglect over the last five years. Yet, I felt a stirring of hope. This girl cared. Despite everything—the lack of food, the violence in her home, the years of placement—Janine had something inside her that called out for love. She was a good daughter. Someone had given her the gift of love when she was younger. And that love was the angel inside that could carry her into a better life.

I was trying to find something to help Janine change from hitting adults and peers and running recklessly into traffic. That meant replacing the open wounds of her life with hope for healing. Janine's smile at the thought of her mother at the door reflected that hope. Janine knew what she wanted. She held fragments of memories tight to her soul: how her mother embraced her, how she had comforted Janine once when she was sick. Janine needed to dismiss the years of neglect and disappointment from her mind. She had no one else.

Looking for a Family

Unlike Janine, Susan, the children's county social worker, had no hope about Janine's mother returning to care for Janine. "Her mother missed 90% of the visits we set up. She forgot Janine's birthday for the last two years. She was nowhere to be found at Christmas. She never went to a drug/alcohol assessment. She never even showed up for the court hearings. Her rights as a parent were terminated," she said. A 12-year history of a mother and a daughter boiled down to a few terse statements of failure and a court ruling. Yet, Janine clutched on to the belief that her mother would return, putting all her faith in a few powerful memories of her mother caring for her and making her world livable, even good—if only briefly when she was very little.

Susan wanted an assessment to determine whether she should continue trying to manage visits between Janine and her two younger siblings. Every time the three children came together, fights quickly broke out. Not just the usual sibling squabbling, but full-scale battles, with lamps and chairs thrown, screaming, and slugging. Typically, Janine and her 9-year-old sister, Ginger, would begin teasing 10-year-old Eddie. I was told that fighting could erupt within minutes.

Eddie had a different father. This man had beaten all of the children and their mother, and was uniformly hated by all three children. Janine and Ginger's father had simply been in and out of their mother's life. A nice smile, a dinner at McDonald's, a good time—now just a fleeting memory with no address, a fading image of a face that Janine didn't even know if she'd recognize any more. He left for the last time when Ginger was just a toddler. No relatives had come forward to contact the children.

Eddie and Ginger were living in a temporary respite home, their third foster family in three years. Their second foster mother had begged Susan to move them elsewhere, telling her, "I can't stand another day with Eddie and Ginger together." Too many fights, too much screaming; it was exhausting. Janine had already been separated from her siblings and sent to a different foster home. Visits with her siblings were temporarily suspended after the three children had ripped furniture, dented walls, and generally trashed the living room of Janine's former group home during their last visit.

Eddie and Ginger had been told that this latest placement was just for a week, to give their second foster mother a break, but I figured the children knew what was coming. They were, by now, veterans of the system. It was doubtful that Janine would be accepted back into any foster home with her two siblings.

Eddie and Ginger were all Janine had left. With that in mind, my crisis residence colleagues and I invited Eddie and Ginger to join us for a sibling visit. Eddie at first sat on Susan's lap, then moved off and sat on the floor across from where Janine was drawing a picture with an assortment of markers. Seconds later, Ginger glared at Eddie. "I hate Eddie, but I like Janine," she taunted.

Janine stared intently at the picture she had started. "Can I have a marker?" Eddie asked her softly.

"I need these," Janine retorted, eyes on her paper, acid in her voice. Eddie squirmed in his seat, a boy without a friend.

Ginger smiled at me, a too-nice smile. I asked her what the rules were for visits with her brother and sister. "I don't know," she mumbled, her smile quickly fading. Ginger saw Susan, leaning forward, poised for the inevitable maelstrom. Ginger looked up, smiled again, and recited a list.

"No yelling. No running. No fighting. No calling names. Follow directions. Don't argue. No blaming. And if anybody disobeys, they have to go to time-out, sit in a chair in the corner, or Susan will hold you." Ginger nodded toward Susan proudly, the picture of a sweet child. *She* certainly wouldn't be the one to cause any trouble.

I asked if the children wanted to see each other in visits. Eddie raised his hand. He had begun drawing a picture with one marker, grudgingly thrust at him by Janine. I looked over to the girls. Ginger, grin in place, was already in motion, climbing over a couch, wrapping her arms around Janine, and slobbering her with wet kisses. If a picture is worth a thousand words, action is worth a chapter. Ginger was answering my question with the drama of her life.

Before I could thank her, Janine giggled and tried to shake Ginger off. Ginger held on, like a rider on a bucking horse. Janine jerked to the left, then to the right, harder and harder, before rolling over on her back, and pinning Ginger against the couch. She could have been a great wrestler, but no one was following any rules for safe competition.

"You can't go!" Ginger screamed.

"Get off of me!" Janine barked.

"No!"

"You brat, I'll knock you out!" Janine's teeth were clenched. She began jerking left and right again. Ginger's head slid closer and closer to the wooden edge of the couch.

"No way!" Ginger squealed, holding on even tighter.

Ginger was revealing much more than the answer to my simple question. Wet kisses led to shoving and slugging. Ginger and Janine reenacted what they had learned about affection in a home with drugs and alcohol. Affection started out sweet, sexy, and intense but ended up dangerous. Janine fought Ginger off as though her life depended on it. I was sure that was part of the girls' experience too.

I would have liked to learn more, but I couldn't expect any verbal answers to my questions. And I didn't want to be liable for the destruction of another office, not to mention the risk to Ginger's head. I asked that Ginger or Janine take a break outside the room with Susan.

"I'll go!" Janine yelled. But Ginger was already rushing past me, leaving a breeze in her wake. In a flash, Ginger was at the door, holding the doorknob and panting loudly with a broad grin.

Giving the girls a choice had obviously been a mistake. They needed safety and guidance. Making choices was a reminder of how they used to live, with no parent in control.

"Why do *I* have to stay?" Janine moaned like a hurt animal being led to the slaughter. Her body slumped down. Her eyes darted angrily at everyone in the room, then locked on mine.

"This always happens," Janine said bitterly. Her voice became sharper as she glared at me. "It's not fair!"

I quickly changed course and said I would see each of the children alone before attempting a combined meeting again. I asked Ginger to stay, figuring she'd be the hardest to get back in the room. Janine and Eddie gladly left with Susan.

Ginger, once again contrite, said she only wanted to see Janine "a little," but would like to see her brother "sometimes." If, in a pretend situation, her mother was to knock on her door, Ginger said she would tell her mother, "Come in."

"Then," she quickly added in a whisper, "I'd leave."

I found Eddie sitting alone, solemnly staring at a television show. He wouldn't look at me, but after a few long minutes he muttered, "I hate my sisters." I tried to learn about his life, but all

I could discover was that Eddie liked his foster mother and had friends in the neighborhood where he lived.

I saw Janine briefly and she agreed to join Eddie and me as he sat staring at the television. Even with Janine in the room, Eddie wouldn't look up.

"He's angry," Janine said.

"Do you know why?" I asked.

"I'm sorry," Janine added, looking at her brother.

Eddie kept staring at the TV. I asked Janine to share with Eddie what she was sorry about.

"For the things I said," Janine whispered. Eddie remained glued to the TV.

"See, you won't listen to me!" Janine snapped and turned her head away from her brother, looking down the hall.

Homeless

Three children with no home and no one, not even each other. Susan had worked hard to at least give them a chance to visit each other, but the children had grown up seeing each other as competitors for their parents' love, rather than as someone to love and be loved by.

Children learn to love by being shown love. These children learned instead that they had to fight for whatever they could find. Ginger seemed to be in the worst position, rejected by her father, mother, and three foster parents. She was desperate for someone to hold her like a baby, a baby who never got the love she craved. She had gotten less from her mother than Eddie or Janine. Everyone had rejected her.

I talked again with Eddie, and after some time he admitted that he'd like to see both his sisters. With my coaxing, Janine returned and said she was sorry again to Eddie. This time Eddie lifted his head and gave her a quick look. It was a start.

I met again with Janine and then with Janine and Ginger, hoping to negotiate some way the children could safely visit each other. Janine, however, balked. She was tired of being squeezed to death by Ginger. Nothing was fair. Eddie was a pain. I asked her to at least say goodbye to her brother and sister.

I coached Ginger to first ask Janine for a hug and not to jump on her sister. I urged the county worker to arrange for dyadic visits, two children at a time. It was all they could handle right now. I felt like a United Nations negotiator, trying to convince warring tribes to accept a peace treaty. No one could predict how long it would last, and nothing was guaranteed.

We brought the children together again to end this visit. Ginger again asked for a hug.

"One kiss and one hug," Janine ordered.

Ginger smiled and lurched forward, reaching out to her sister, almost jumping into her arms. I feared Janine would jump back or punch her. Instead, she put her arms around Ginger. Ginger began to rock back and forth in a gentle rhythm, her head nestled into Janine's shoulder, both girls oblivious to the class going on nearby or the adults around them. And Janine held on. Two girls, arms wrapped around each other, swaying to music only they knew. Two abandoned children reaching out for everything they had lost.

Grieving a Lost Mother

Janine was placed at our crisis residence for the usual reasons— "Dangerous to self and others," "Unsafe in less restrictive care." These were the state's criteria for admission. She had assaulted staff at her group home and darted into traffic as she ran away from one foster or group home after another. Her message was clear: "No one can give me what I need. Why should I listen to any of you or do anything you say?"

The judge may have given up, but for Janine and her siblings, only their mother's last message remained. "She told us she'd get us back," Janine whispered to me.

How do you find love and give love when you are 12 years old and feel like everything has been ripped away from you? Ginger's desperate lunge reminded Janine of all she missed in her life and the empty and aching feeling the children shared deep inside. She could never replace their wishes for a mother.

How do you grieve the loss of someone who is still alive? Our culture gives us little guidance. There was no gravestone to mark the end of Janine's mother. No wake, funeral, or unveiling. No one sat shiva with the children for a week at a relative's home. I would have liked to prescribe any or all of these customs. The pain of abandonment is surely worse than death. Janine and her siblings knew that their mother had chosen drugs and boyfriends over her children.

The county would continue to look for an adoptive family. The children needed parents who could accept their past, their longing for their mother, their loyalty to her, and their anger at her abandonment. I urged the county worker to renew a search for Aunt Rose. If nothing else, Janine might gain a chance to learn more about her mother or have a chance to grieve with a relative and possibly to send a message through relatives to her mother.

Before she could grieve, Janine needed to give up trying to find her mother. It was not enough that county workers had looked for her mother. Janine had to feel that she had done her best and that everyone had tried their hardest to help her mom. Janine didn't believe that yet.

No One Makes It Alone

I remembered Janine's quiet joy at the thought of her mother coming to visit her, knocking on her door. On that dark day, with no one around her she could trust, Janine could still smile. And her smile revealed the hidden side of Janine, the caring daughter and sister.

Our job was to pull out that smile, rekindle Janine's hope, and help all three children get the embraces, the love, they needed. Today's visit for the three children was only a tiny piece of the work that needed to take place. Yet, even in this forced intervention, an evaluation of the siblings' ability to visit together, we had learned an important lesson.

I saw it in Ginger's desperate lunge at her sister, her slobbering kisses. She was crying out for someone to love her in the only way she remembered. Eddie reacted in just the opposite way to his sisters, giving up and withdrawing into a stone-like and impenetrable silence. He created walls to keep the others out and protect the little he had. By most standards, Janine was the most disturbed, the most at risk. Yet, she had shown the greatest honesty and strength of all the children.

Janine had asked me, "Why should I see you?" What did I have to offer three children, abandoned by their fathers and extended family, and chained to memories and imperatives to remain loyal to their drug-addicted mother, a mother who, I believed, had taught Janine that love was precious but fleeting, and worth fighting, even dying for? The county social services department had no family willing to take these three children. Janine had already been removed once again from a family's home and placed in group care. She certainly did not want to hear anything I might tell her to do. I had no magic spell that would make up for her years of loss and neither the strength nor the courage to raise Janine or her siblings myself.

Yet, in her heart, Janine knew the answer to her question. She needed the embrace that she gave to her little sister. Janine could learn to be a sister and shed the burden of acting as a substitute mother. If the children could only be together two at a time, for one hug, it was a start, slow and safe. Each hug marked a chance to reaffirm their identity in a fractured world, a chance to grieve, to hold on, however briefly, to someone who knew the aching each of them felt inside, and a chance to rekindle the caring they had lost.

In *Peter Pan*, the fairy, Tinkerbell, grows stronger or weaker with every child who believes in her. If no one believes, she dies. I believe attachments work the same way for children, and in fact, for all of us. One stable relationship with a person who cares for and values a child can keep that child growing and help that child survive. Janine, alone and seemingly with only the clothes on her back, was not lost.

Turning Points

Janine came into our crisis residence with no one. Abandoned by her parents and unable to even visit with her siblings, she had become a destructive force. It would be an illusion to pretend that we can create miracles with children like Janine, and somehow restore everything they have lost in their lives. But we can begin to rebuild the vital relationships these children need to survive.

Janine needed family members to love and who would love her. In her short time in the crisis residence, we helped her begin to reestablish contact with her siblings. Janine and her siblings began weekly visits with each other, two children at a time, starting with short, 30-minute visits. No more rooms were destroyed.

We also contacted Janine's aunt and birthfather following our meeting. Her aunt began to visit Janine twice a month, giving her a renewed sense of family. Sadly, the children's birthfather, like their mother, made no effort to change his life and provide a home for Janine or her siblings. Eventually, the county department of social services filed a petition to terminate the rights of Janine's birthfather based on his failure to make any effort to help the children. Freeing Janine and her siblings for adoption gave Janine the chance to move into a permanent family, rather than having to grow up moving in and out of temporary group homes or foster families.

Janine did well enough in the crisis residence to be referred to a foster family. Yet Janine could not believe that her mother did not want her back, and she resisted moving into another family. She was transferred to a group care program, ran away three times, and eventually found her mother on the street. County workers had been unable to find Janine's mother, but Janine tracked her down herself.

Janine tried once more to convince her mother to rebuild the family, begging her mother to take her with her. But Janine's mother turned away from Janine, back to her drugs and her "friends." This time, Janine realized that her mother couldn't care for her children. The mother she loved was gone. Janine had struggled with all her might to win her mother's love and failed.

But Janine did not give up on love. "I want a family," Janine told her social worker. She did well in her program and moved into a foster family who eventually adopted her.

For children in crisis, threatening or anguished behaviors cover the frayed or broken threads of their attachments to parents, siblings, and other people whom they have loved. Our job as parents, teachers, neighbors, and therapists begins with learning how to listen. Children may tell adults what they think we want to hear, what a family member told them to say, what they think will frighten us away, or they may tell us nothing at all. But, if we are patient enough and strong enough, I have found that even the angriest children are looking for opportunities to tell caring adults what they need to know to help their families and themselves. We just have to prove ourselves. Can we listen closely to a child's very breath, the intonation of her voice, her shrieks of joy and terror, her sudden silences, her laughter and grief? Can we read a child's body language around the important people in his life, decipher his furtive glances, learn who he reaches to for comfort and protection? Can we take the time to let a child tell his story in play, narrative, music, or motion? By validating children's love *and* their pain, we can open up pathways to the angels buried deep inside. Janine, the assaulter of nuns, was underneath it all a loyal and loving daughter and sibling, seeking comfort in a lonely world.

The yearning for attachment marks our basic humanity. If Janine and her siblings could care for and support each other, those of us who are blessed with so much can also overcome the stigmas and old habits that keep us apart from members of our own families. What worked for Janine and her siblings points the way to steps we all can take to improve our lives and protect our loved ones.

VANESSA

Our lives begin to end the day we become silent
about the things that matter.

–Dr. Martin Luther King Jr.

*V*anessa tightened her cheeks, clenched her jaw, and gave each of us sitting around the table a silent glare. It was a look of clear disdain specially designed for her mother, her social worker, her foster mother, and me, as if to say, in no uncertain terms, "You guys just don't get it!"

We were talking about expanding Vanessa's visits with Gloria, her mother. Vanessa had just spent a year in a foster home, and Gloria had finally completed the first phase of an outpatient alcohol-counseling program. Vanessa wanted overnight visits with her mother in a home she could call her own.

"Soon, honey. As soon as I can find another job," Gloria said softly.

The adults in the room were content to go along with Gloria's plan. Gloria's alcohol treatment counselors had praised her progress, and we wanted to give her every chance to change a lifetime of drinking.

Vanessa had spoken thus far in our meeting with a soft, whiny voice, like an irritable little girl who wasn't getting her way. But, after hearing her mother's response, Vanessa's entire countenance changed. Her voice deepened and took on an edge.

"I don't *want* to go home for just a few hours. I *need* a longer time to be with my mother. I *need* to be able to see her whenever I *want.*"

Vanessa was declaring her manifesto. It was more than a petulant demand from an angry child. She was declaring what she needed and had never known.

Gloria had spent Vanessa's childhood working nights at bars, serving beer and drinking beer, consumed with her own problems. Her daughter spent most of her free time and most nights with her grandmother. When her grandmother became ill, Vanessa found herself living with her father and an aunt. She felt unwanted by everyone. At age 13, Vanessa was already involved with a group of girls who stole from stores and broke into houses. She was tired of waiting for her mother to change her night job, the job that had led to her drinking problem, the job she continued to hold even after six months of alcohol counseling. Vanessa had heard her mother talk about changing jobs for years and years. She knew every line, every promise.

Vanessa didn't want a part-time mom who looked good at her weekly individual and group therapy sessions and during their two-hour weekly visits. She wanted a parent, 24 hours a day, seven days a week, month after month. Vanessa had learned that she couldn't trust Gloria to be there when she was sick or hurt, or just needed a snuggle. Who could comfort her when her friends turned their backs or a teacher snapped at her? If her mom had not been available for the last 13 years and couldn't be available now, why should she believe in her mother in the future? Vanessa wanted a mother who cared enough to help her at any time, day or night.

Vanessa was described as a "problem child," but I admired the courage it took to assert her needs and demand that the adults in her life, including the professionals, face the truth. And the truth was, she couldn't wait any longer. Her mother had been making choices hour by hour, day by day, and night by night throughout Vanessa's life. Every day and night that her mother was out drinking or working at the bar sent a message to Vanessa, a message that she could not depend on her mother.

I looked at Vanessa and felt my eyes opening wider. We talked about the pain of waiting, what Vanessa needed, and how little time was left for a 13-year-old. Vanessa needed a mother, and she needed her mother to act now.

Vanessa reminded me that it's not about spoken words or promises. Children can only wait a short time. Each week is precious. Each day shows a child whether Mom, Dad, Grandma, or Grandpa really cares. The tasks and challenges change as the child grows up, but the basic premise remains the same: Parenting is the hard stuff, the real stuff. And children like Vanessa show all of us the difference between fantasy and reality.

JON

*The past does have a life of its own, and it will
walk into your house and sit at your table
and call itself something else, unless you're
willing to look at it in truth.*

–Oprah Winfrey
From an interview on Toni Morrison's Beloved

*T*wo boys sped through the half-dark parking garage, far be-
low the marble pillars and the mahogany-paneled chambers of
the state's capitol. Jon sported an earring, mostly hidden beneath
curly blonde hair and a navy Yankees baseball cap yellowed around
the edges with sweat and dirt. A few freckles sparkled on his
nose. His face was lean, matching his wiry body. Skinny legs pumped
hard on the pedals of a bike too small by half for his size.

Jon trailed closely behind Ted, his new best friend. Ted was
taller, with broad shoulders and a ripped, sleeveless T-shirt featur-
ing a rap artist recently shot and killed. Ted had ended the school
year suspended for punching a teacher. He had a winning smile
and a quick temper. Together, Jon and Ted had spent their first
four weeks of summer vacation cruising through the city on

their bikes, swiping candy and sodas from convenience stores, and staying out late, as late as they pleased.

Ted headed for the loading docks. It was quiet today in the parking garage, almost eerie in the dim light. The loading platforms were stacked with boxes from a nearby truck, but strangely, no one was around.

Ted grinned and looked over his shoulder at Jon following behind. "We're in!"

Jon hoisted himself onto the dock, closely following Ted. A surge of energy shot through his veins. Exploring with Ted made him feel alive. He loved the danger of almost getting caught and the thrill of pulling a fast one on adults. Jon hated anyone who gave orders, made rules, or tried to stifle him. Maybe that's why he had wanted to check out the capitol building's garage today. Whatever the suits and skirts did up there in their marble offices, Jon knew it didn't help him.

Ted surveyed the loading docks quickly. Two trucks, a stack of cartons, a long workbench, and some garbage in the corner. A rusty 10-gallon can with the word "gasoline" sat on the floor by the workbench. Without a word, Ted bent over the can and tried to shake it.

"It's loaded," he called out to Jon. "Help me lift it!"

Twisting the cap, Ted sniffed and grinned again.

"Come on!" he urged Jon. Side by side, the two boys strained to lift the heavy can.

"Over there!" Ted pointed with his head. The boys stumbled toward the truck.

"That's close enough." Ted ordered.

Together, the boys tilted the can and began to pour the golden liquid in spirals, around and around, forming an ever-widening puddle. "Awesome!" Ted beamed when the last drops reached the truck. He pulled out his lighter, flicked the igniter, and tossed it into the puddle.

Just then, the loading dock foreman returned to the docks. Jon and Ted watched the lighter flicker in the puddle.

"I'm outta here!" Ted cried as he jumped on his bike.

Jon turned. The foreman blocked his path to his bike. He ran to the right, trying to evade him, but the man grabbed his arms and pulled him into a headlock. Jon gasped for air. The man's arms slid down around his chest. Jon felt like he was being crushed. He gasped for air and struggled to break free. Jon looked wildly around him, hoping Ted would return to help him, but Ted was nowhere to be seen.

Desperately, Jon scanned the parking garage, straining against the man's body. Out of the corner of his eye, he saw the puddle glistening in the neon light.

"Stop it!" the man ordered.

Jon jerked his head toward the puddle and stared, transfixed. Jon's heart pounded louder and harder within him. The man was saying something but Jon couldn't hear.

Jon spotted the lighter. His face stiffened. Jon stopped struggling and watched as the tiny flame flickered, then died.

Another Chance

I met Jon three weeks later in our crisis residence. The police report was brief. "Suspect poured flammable fluid in parking garage. Attempted to set fire with lighter. When confronted, suspect denied involvement, blamed friend and explained gasoline on his sneakers by saying he slipped in the gasoline while watching his friend. Said his friend wanted to set the capitol garage on fire. Suspect later admitted pouring 'some gasoline.'"

Jon and Ted almost made the next day's headlines. If the fluid had ignited, the boys would almost certainly have burned to death in the resulting explosion. The fire would have likely destroyed two trucks and a car, and severely damaged the parking garage, according to the investigator's report. A mistake had saved Jon and Ted. They didn't realize that the "gasoline" can didn't actually contain gasoline but another fluid, flammable but not so easily ignited.

Ted was placed on probation, ordered to participate in counseling, and remanded to the custody of his father. It was his first offense, and the judge heeded his father's plea to let him off lightly. Jon, however, had been before the court two years earlier for setting a neighbor's house on fire, hitting a girl with a stick, running away from school, and defying his mother. The judge scowled as she read over Jon's record. Four previous placements, 10 fires in and around his home, and just recently, he had broken windows in a school bus. Jon was ordered into placement for an evaluation and pending disposition. He was 10 years old.

If Jon had been three years older, he would have been sent off to serve an 18-month sentence in a locked facility for juvenile delinquents. Five years older and he would very likely have been sent to prison. The judge and probation officer wanted to give Jon another chance to change his life and more help than would be possible in detention. But Jon had already received a greater blessing. By escaping from the fire, he had been granted another chance at life itself.

Search and Rescue

I shuddered as I read the description of Jon's firesetting. By all accounts, this boy would have been incinerated. Next time, Jon would know how to find the real gasoline, if not something more dangerous. I knew I was feeling the threat inherent in Jon and Ted's behavior, a message of fear spiraling outward.

When the fear and danger in a child's behavior begin to affect me, I know I have to back up and find a way to keep myself safe so I can join with family members and colleagues to do something helpful. It's easy to jump to conclusions, throw out labels, and prescribe generic interventions like "residential treatment," "detention," or "family therapy"—recommendations that leave the pain and the work to someone else. Instead, I wanted to use what Jon was showing us.

Firesetting often reflects a quest for power, the thrill of the flame, and a flirtation with death. Although Ted had a lot to do with this particular fire, we needed to focus on Jon's series of fires, look for patterns, and not get lost in the details of any one incident. Dangerous behaviors often echo over time like an ominous drumbeat. I wanted to look for repeated themes in Jon's defiant behavior and follow the rhythm of his actions to what needed to change. What led up to his setting a fire? Who was there? Who was missing in his life? What did he feel inside? What was he thinking about himself? I knew we did not have to operate in the dark. Children who set fires are often threatened from a young age by abandonment and family violence. This shapes their beliefs, their ability to manage frustration, and their identities. Was this true for Jon? Did he feel abandoned at key points in his life? Was there violence in his home? Most important, who could help Jon to heal and rebuild the safety, nurturance, and predictability he would need to change?

Safety would have to be our first goal: keeping Jon safe, keeping the family safe, and keeping the community safe. Jon needed help to defuse the triggers to his rage, to provide the safety he needed, and to teach him how to get his needs met without exploding.

Man of the House

I respect the competence, the concern, and the power of family members. I learned long ago to join with a family whenever possible and help them tap into their own strengths, rather than trying to change them with techniques or interventions. Instead of endowing one therapist and one weekly, hour-long session with the primary responsibility for effecting change, my colleagues and I invited those who cared about Jon to work together with us.

I met Jon with his mother, Bev; his mother's new boyfriend, Stan; his family therapist; and a case manager appointed by the county mental health department. Jon sat on the floor next to his mother, looking up at her frequently, but saying little. At my request, he sketched a picture of how he saw his family. He pictured "Mommy," Stan, and himself smiling beneath ponderous clouds. Dark drops of rain poured down on everyone. Jon conspicuously left his two younger sisters, Georgette (age 8) and Alicia (age 5) out of his family drawing, and his mother had chosen not to bring them to our meeting.

I looked to Bev and asked if it would be okay for Jon to share what he remembered from when he was younger. Bev began swinging her leg back and forth in a rocking motion. "Yeah," she mumbled in an almost inaudible voice. "Why isn't Ted placed?" Bev quickly added, her voice becoming louder but weighted with bitterness. "Why is he still living at home? That boy thumbs his nose at me!" Not surprisingly, Jon said nothing for the first half-hour of our meeting.

I knew that we could spend an hour eliciting details about the fire or discussing the inequities in how the two boys were being treated by family court, but this had already been explored by Jon's probation officer. This was only the latest episode in a series of increasingly dangerous incidents in which Jon had been involved. The clearest messages from a child can be found when they first begin to get into trouble. Later acts reflect layers of problems and the effects (positive and negative) of peers, family members, authorities, and service providers that often obscure the factors driving a child to risk his life or the lives of others. For Jon, that meant going back to the first fire he set, the first time he risked his life playing with the power of matches to change a bad situation. He'd set the sheets on his bed on fire. At the time, he was 3 years old.

Bev gradually relaxed after I assured her that I didn't believe in blaming anyone, parents or children. We needed to look for what could help Jon. Bev shared how Ralph, Jon's father, beat her throughout their relationship.

"I was stuck in the house," Bev said tersely, each word pointed and angry. I wondered what it would be like for a boy to grow up listening to the rancor in her voice day after day. How could Jon find a way to feel good about himself with so much bitterness all around him?

I tried to find out what had attracted her to Jon's father. Why did she pick him out of all the men she knew? Jon needed to know what strengths he could draw from his father.

"I didn't have nobody," Bev replied, a tear forming in her eye. "I did it to get loved. I couldn't stay with my mom and her dope-fiend boyfriend. My grandmother reared me until I was 13, but then she died and I went to live with my mother." For Bev, that meant living with drugs, men in and out of her mother's home, and beatings by her mother when she tried to sneak away. "Then Ralph beat me, even before Jon was born," Bev went on. Ralph was Bev's ticket out of her mother's home, but she ended up in greater danger than ever. "He used to threaten to kill me." Bev's lips pursed and quivered as she remembered Ralph charging toward her with a knife. "When Jon was 5, I had to get a friend to go after him."

"I watch my mama's back!" Jon interjected.

Bev and I both looked down in surprise at Jon's sudden entrance into our conversation. Earlier, his voice had been a soft, barely audible mumble as he bent over his drawing. He had hardly acknowledged my presence. Now, he looked me squarely in the eye and spoke loudly with an edge in his voice.

"How do you do that?" I asked. I was impressed with the strength of his voice, bold and just as bitter as his mother's was.

"Anyone messes with my mother, I tell 'em, 'You better leave my mother alone!'" This was a boy with a mission. He would protect his mother with all his might and watch over her forever.

Jon said he didn't remember the fight with the knife his mother had described, but he did remember his mother getting hurt and his father yelling, "I'll kill you!"

"He tried to cut my mother with a razor." Jon stared at his mother and their eyes locked. "I remember the blood coming out, all over his thumb. He cut himself."

According to Bev, Jon was 3 years old at the time.

When I saw him alone, Jon shared with me that his father had not only beat his mother, but had also hit Jon and Georgette "with anything he could get his hands on." Worse, Jon recalled how his father cursed them, "Damn you kids!" he'd yell. Ralph would come home drunk, said Jon, scream at the kids if they weren't in bed, and chase them into their rooms.

Bev didn't believe Ralph had hurt the children. "It was just me," Bev insisted. "And I'll never let any man do that again."

It was a declaration of strength, and I admired the resolve in her voice.

"What did Jon do when you and his father were fighting?" I asked Bev.

"He'd try to get in between us. Ralph would tell him, 'Go sit down, Jon.'"

"Then what would happen?" I asked softly. Jon looked up at his mother.

"Jon would go in the corner, sit down, and cry," Bev answered. I could see Jon staring down at the floor.

"I'm not afraid of him anymore," said Bev, glancing at Stan, her new boyfriend. "Not as long as I have a man with me."

"And when I don't have a man, Jon becomes the man of the house," she added with a smile.

I asked Jon what he did when he acted as "man of the house."

Jon sat up, straightened his back, and paused for a moment. "Take care of the house, take care of the family," he replied. His voice became deeper, husky but terse, more like a man of 40 who had been through a lot of tough times than a young boy of 10.

I asked Bev how she saw Jon taking care of the family.

"He tells me, 'No men!'" she replied with a flicker of a grin. Jon mirrored his mother's smile.

"We're getting married in a month," Stan interjected. Jon's smile disappeared.

Later, when I asked the couple to draw pictures of their own showing how they saw the family, Stan drew Bev as pregnant and happy. Bev drew herself in eight months, going to the park with her two girls, Jon, Stan, and a new baby. Smiling at the thought, Bev looked fondly at Stan.

Jon turned back to his drawings, but I felt a pit in my stomach. Conception of the new baby must have taken place around the same time Jon was trying to set the garage on fire. Bev had not heard her son.

During a meeting we had a few days later, Bev minimized Jon's problems. She believed that he simply had to stop chasing after boys like Ted. "He just needs to listen to me," she said. "That's all!" Bev also discounted Jon's claim that his previous one-year placement in residential treatment had been because his mother needed a break from him.

I asked Jon if his mother had changed. "No," he had solemnly replied, his head down. "She doesn't keep her promises."

Three months after Jon's return from residential treatment, Stan had returned from a drug treatment program. Bev sent the children to an aunt's home for the night.

"Jon must have stolen the key to my apartment. Then he snuck back in during the middle of the night," Bev complained. Jon had found Stan and her in bed having sex. "He stormed out," she continued angrily. "He shouldn't have been there in the first place. It's *not* my fault!"

"Then, at 3:00 in the morning, I find him standing over me! I was just sleeping. I yelled at him to get out! He ran downstairs. I found him in the kitchen. That's when he threw the pot at me and called me a name. He started hitting me." Bev's voice rose in pitch, stern now, and shrill. She glared at Jon. "No boy's going to hit me!"

Bev called the mobile crisis unit from the county mental health department. Jon was placed into a local psychiatric hospital for three weeks, then returned to his mother.

"After that, he wouldn't listen to me," Bev said. "I told him to stay in the yard. He went chasing after Ted. It's not my fault!" Bev repeated.

Three months later, Jon tried to set the capitol garage on fire.

Lighting a Fire Under the State

Ironically, just two years before Jon visited the capitol, the governor had slashed spending on direct social service programs for families like Jon's, including a $10 million cut from the child protective budget of the county Jon lived in. At the same time, the state funded locked facilities for delinquents, group homes, and private psychiatric hospitals. In other words, the state's leaders provided funding to hold children found to be dangerous in institutions, for workers to complete case reports, and for staff to provide "stabilization," but very little in the way of prevention. Few to no services existed to help parents protect their children from poverty and violence, for example, or to help family members overcome traumas.

Our crisis residence was designed to help children who had been dangerous to themselves or others with a fraction of the state funding reserved for psychiatric hospitals or locked facilities. We had a long waiting list of children who needed immediate respite from their families, as well as assessments and family interventions. The program had operated with a large deficit since its inception and depended on donations of time and funding from the agency to provide psychological evaluations, family interventions, and trauma work.

State regulations prohibited funding one child for more than 21 days in the crisis residence unless state regulators granted an appeal for additional time. As funding grew tighter, regulators pressed harder for all children to leave the residence by the 21-day limit. For families like Jon's with longstanding problems, this often meant moving the child to one or more additional facilities before allowing him or her to return home. Family members needed to tell their stories to another set of practitioners and test again to see if they would be helped or shamed. In the process, they learned that service providers are temporary. Jon could be kept off the streets and out of the capitol's parking garage temporarily, but providing needed services over time would be a struggle.

As soon as he, his mother, and others in their lives could move beyond the old traumas, I believed Jon should go home. If he didn't, the standard court order for delinquent youth like Jon was another year in an institution. I worried that if this happened, Jon and his mother would see this as a year to serve a "sentence," a message from the judge that Jon was "bad" and that Bev was right to be angry with him. Then, after a year of placement, Jon would go back to a mother who would be absorbed with raising her new baby. His losses would be compounded, his bond to Bev further weakened.

At this point, however, Jon remained too caught up in the helplessness he had felt for so long, and he showed too many warning signs of unspoken anger and an inability to control his firesetting impulses, to be able to return home safely. The thrill of setting fires had become an addiction in itself. If Jon was signaling for help, he had not yet been answered.

Losing It All

Children who set fires often begin when they feel they are losing everything and everybody, when they cannot even pretend to feel the love the they had counted on, and their nightmares of monsters penetrate into the daylight. These children often become fixated within the time when the level of violence in the home reaches the point where they believe that someone will die. This level of trauma frequently occurs if a child sees blood coupled with threats by a parent or another important adult to kill the other parent. The child's basic trust is lost, and he or she feels angry and alone. Getting into trouble brings attention and a sense that the child has at least some control in the midst of disaster, but this fleeting power comes with a heavy cost. The anger in the family becomes channeled toward the child, and discipline in the form of beatings and curses may cement the message to the child that he or she is unwanted. Children may become homeless long before they physically leave their families.

Jon told me he kept remembering the time his father cut his thumb and he saw his father's blood. He couldn't get it out of his head. That was the same year he set the sheets on his bed on fire. I asked him mother what she thought. "Just an accident," Bev said. "Just a boy playing with matches. I keep telling him not to do it!"

I showed Jon a picture of a girl looking sad and asked Jon to make up a story. Jon said the girl was going to get a whipping. Her mother would tell the girl to "turn around, close your eyes, and start crying." Bev and Stan both believed in whippings for children. Jon looked at the ceiling as he finished his story, and his voice softened and rose slightly in pitch, like a little boy chanting a rhyme: "Run away, run away, run away until next year," he sang.

Jon drew a picture of a boy for me and made up a little song. "Feeling something neat…running down the street." The rap ended with the boy "lookin' to get killed."

"Why does he want to get killed?" I asked.

"Because he hates his father," Jon replied. "His father is so mean!"

Jon believed deep inside that he was so bad that he might as well be dead. His father's curses and beatings were proof. Unfortunately, nothing much had changed since Jon was 3. He had tried his best to "watch his mama's back," but she had moved on in her life, and as she became more and more desperate and enraged by his defiance, she had most likely come to beat Jon herself. Bev, in her own desperation, had ended up acting like Ralph.

Changing the Story

Hell in one Jewish tradition is a place where people are unspeakably cruel to each other, literally the valley where human sacrifices are held.* Jon had been shaped by a world where no one answered the cries of his mother in her own youth or as a young woman. I visualized 3-year-old Jon crumpled against the wall, tears

---

* From Wolpe, D. J. (1993). *Teaching your children about God*. New York: Henry Holt and Co.

streaming down his cheeks while his father tried to cut up his mother, a picture of helplessness and despair. No one had answered Jon's tears. He cried alone, and in those moments, Jon's spirit changed. This bright, loving little boy learned that crying did no good. It was no wonder that matches and fire held such an appeal.

Jon still spoke and acted with the words, beliefs, and feelings of this 3-year-old. He needed his mother's help and the help of others the family could trust to help him move on. When Jon told his rhyming stories ("run away, run away"), he slid back before my eyes to the age when he felt he lost his mother and his father, the time of his first fire. To help Jon and his mother meant going back to when he was 3 and changing Jon's life story. He needed to feel the antidote to his father's curse, "Damn you!" and the bloody attacks on his mother. Most of all, Jon needed to rebond to his mother in a different way, as a son who could feel loved as a son, and not just her guardian.

Helping a firesetting youth means looking for the loving side of a child, the side that is still fighting to reclaim the nurturing that was lost. It was hard to see Jon, the firesetter, as an angel, but if we traced his tears to his worst pain and listened closely to his proud assertions about being "the man of the house," you could plainly hear his plea. Jon was his mother's guardian. And he truly believed he had failed his greatest responsibility.

I wondered how Jon could get the care he needed as a 10-year-old. How could he find a positive role to replace the necessity he had felt growing up to guard his mother night and day? He would need to see that his mother was protecting herself without Jon watching over her at 3:00 in the morning, that she would have the energy to set and enforce rules without whippings, and that she could provide for the family. This was a tall order for a single mother, pregnant with her fourth child, and receiving no child support, but Jon's chances seemed slight if Bev could not help her son move beyond his mission in life to "watch her back."

Bev needed to take charge of her son. That meant getting the help she needed to watch him, nurture him, discipline him, and care for him as both a 3-year-old and a 10-year-old. She needed to raise him up from the point he became stuck feeling he had failed her. Jon needed to learn other ways to be a winner—in the sports he loved, for example—and to manage frustrations without setting fires or running away from his mother. They could help each other.

I shared the police report with Bev. It emphasized that Jon would have been killed if the fluid he and Ted tried to ignite had actually been gasoline. Bev didn't think she could keep Jon from leaving her home or yard, but insisted that he had to come home. I told Bev I agreed that he needed his family, but at this point, Jon could not believe that anything was different at home. He still saw his mother as too depressed to care for or discipline him, and would certainly not be able to trust the new man in her life for a long time.

Bev listened and her face tensed. "I want my son. He's coming home to me. I'm going to court!" She began to cry. Jon quickly moved to her side, sitting close, leaning toward his mother and looking up at her tear-filled eyes. Jon's cheeks were drawn, a hurt look in his own eyes.

"What do I need to do?" Jon pleaded to his mother.

Bev looked down through her tears.

"What do I need to do?" Jon pleaded again, this time looking at me.

Jon still craved his mother's love. He was, above all, a loyal son. Staff at the crisis residence liked him, and he reciprocated the attention he received, doing well in school and in activities. He could be a model child. To me, that meant that Jon had gotten love from someone, most likely his mother. "I'm glad you are going to fight to bring Jon home," I said to Bev. "I don't think either of you were to blame for what happened when Jon was 3 years old, when his father tried to kill you."

Jon showed us that he could change his behavior when he had adults who could see the tears he shed. With permission to be honest with his mother and support for Bev in place, we could challenge Jon to choose between acting like a 3-year-old or a 10-year-old. Ten-year-olds who act like 3-year-olds have to be watched all the time to keep them safe. That's what Jon's firesetting demanded of us. Either his family and community helpers could put together a team of guardians to supervise him all day, or he would have to live in a group care center with professional staff watching over him until he and his family could change. Over time, he could earn the rights and privileges of a 10-year-old.

To prove he was able to function as a 10-year-old, Jon also needed to take responsibility for what he had done and make amends. This did not mean serving a fixed sentence, like a criminal incarcerated for his crimes. Jon needed to apologize for his actions and make restitution in whatever way was possible. This could include cleaning up the mess he made in the parking garage, helping to unload trucks, or working for money that would be sent to a firemen's fund. Ideally, Jon's restitution would include the staff at the parking garage. He also needed to apologize to his mother and with her help find a way to make up for the agony he put her through.

The next steps would be even harder. Jon needed to see that his mother acknowledged her own responsibility for not caring for Jon when she was caught up in marital violence and her own depression. She needed to replace her shame with pride in what she was doing. But this still would not be enough. No one can rebuild trust overnight, especially a child who learned as a 3-year-old that he couldn't trust his mother.

Side by Side

Jon cried softly, his sighs rhythmically tied to those of his mother. I looked at Jon and his mother, united again in their tears. I knew that Jon could feel his mother's pain, and that he would fear losing her again.

Jon and Bev had been teetering on the edge of grieving all that they had lost. By grieving together, they could begin to move out of the past and change. I was reminded of my own losses, my father's death so many years ago, and the crying I held off for so many years. It took me years to get over my own fear of crying and to release my own grief. I wished I could magically remove their anguish and promise them a happy ending, but I knew that Jon and Bev needed to feel the pain of their losses before they could help each other.

I held myself back and watched silently. This was a precious moment for Jon and Bev, not to be encumbered. A few minutes went by and neither made any effort to break apart. I felt a small stirring of hope as I watched Bev and Jon cry together, side by side, as they leaned into each other.

"I'm not going to give you up. No man is going to get in between us." Bev whispered.

She told Jon that she could protect herself. She started counseling for her own depression and eventually was able to bring Jon back into her home.

Tears traced Jon and Bev's bitterness *and* their love, both buried under the guise of anger. For a moment, the cloak of anger was cast aside. Jon and Bev had a chance to embrace and move beyond the battles. I admired their courage in letting themselves break down and cry. Fragile as it was, Jon and Bev were rebuilding their bond to each other, a bond linked in their tears.

Jon and his mother got another chance, and Jon continued to do well in the crisis residence. In family counseling, Jon told his mother again how he felt he had to protect her. Jon and Bev cried again talking about the fire. Bev knew she had almost lost her son. Bev eventually supported Jon's move into a group care program to help him learn how to deal with his frustrations in a more adaptive way. We arranged for a mentor to begin helping Jon and to provide a model for how men could manage frustrations. The residential program provided a therapist who worked with Bev and her family. Jon became connected to a child care staff member he liked.

Learning from Jon

Losses magnify from generation to generation. Bev lost her grandmother and ended up with no one caring for her at age 14. She became a battered mother. Jon essentially lost his father and his mother to violence. In his experience, fathers represented hitting, curses, abandonment, and prison. Mothers represented injury, depression, and rejection. By age 8, Jon had given up on getting help within his family and moved on to set his fires in the neighborhood. By age 10, Jon had sounded the alarm bell at the state capitol itself.

Jon showed me once again how a sensitive, caring little boy lives or dies by the love he gets from his parents and those who care for him. A 3-year-old who is rejected by both his mother and his father will feel like dying. A 3-year-old who witnesses violence repeatedly will learn to become just as violent against himself and everyone else. Perhaps this is the worst aspect of the hell created in violent families. Hidden and ignored, the curse of violence infects families and neighborhoods. The curses and cruelty pass from generation to generation, spiraling outward until someone listens and stops the violence.

But children have an amazing ability to heal: Consider the power of a kiss, a hug, and a magic Band-Aid, an adult willing to feel their pain and show them how the world can be safe again. A home with regular routines for waking up, going to school, mealtimes, and bedtime. These are the simple but powerful rituals that make a child's world predictable and safe. Jon still needed someone to pick him up, kiss away his tears, and show him that an adult saw what scared him and would make things better. My colleagues and I had shown Jon and his mother that together, we could face the old horrors, and we weren't going to sugarcoat a life-or-death crisis. Crying together that day reawakened the nightmares they shared, but painful as it was, Jon and Bev did not collapse or die. Jon learned that his mother cared enough to cry for what they both had lost. In our sessions, Jon and Bev's sighs replaced the drumbeats of rage and fear.

PART II

Children Transcending

Trauma

11

RODNEY

*If you want to raise a man from mud and filth,
do not think it is enough to keep standing on top
and reaching down to give a helping hand.
You must go all the way down yourself, down into
mud and filth. Then take hold with strong hands and
pull him and yourself into the light."*

–Solomon ben Meir ha-Levi of Karlin

Thirteen-year-old Rodney secretly kept a pocketknife under his pillow. When Sue Clary, his foster mother, discovered the knife, the boy insisted that he couldn't sleep without it. Instead of grabbing the knife, lecturing Rodney on the need to give up all weapons, or chastising the boy for feeling scared and disrespecting the family's rules, Sue replied that she understood. She knew that Rodney had lived a lifetime with physical and sexual violence, especially at night. He had no reason to trust.

Sue asked Rodney if he would please, for her sake, keep a whistle under his pillow instead of the knife. She promised him that she and her husband would respond to the whistle at any hour and protect him. She also urged Rodney to test the whistle to prove to himself that he could depend on his foster parents to be there when he needed them.

Rodney eventually agreed to exchange his knife for the whistle. One night, in an emergency, he tested whether Sue and her husband would keep their promise. They did. And gradually, Rodney learned that there were some people in the world he could trust enough to make a new life.

I have enormous admiration for adults willing to take children into their homes and provide care and supervision on a 24-hour-a-day basis. We ask foster parents to care for the same children whom state authorities and HMOs have just certified as requiring round-the-clock supervision by teams of professionals in private hospitals or secure detention facilities. Practitioners like me go home at the end of the day. Substitute parents can't leave. When children have experienced threats and pain throughout their lives, it's almost a given that they will test the adults around them to see if their new home can really be different than the way they used to live. Foster and adoptive parents have to be willing to prove themselves consistently and repeatedly if they truly want to help children rebuild their faith in themselves and in the adults in their lives. Not only that, but being a foster or adoptive parent also means caring enough to validate a child's love for another parent and being strong enough to weather the child's pain. It's hard to trust again.

TODD

Listen to the mustn'ts, child
Listen to the don'ts,
Listen to the shouldn'ts
The impossibles, the won'ts
Listen to the never haves
Then listen close to me—
ANYTHING can happen, child
ANYTHING can be. *

–Shel Silverstein
Where the Sidewalk Ends

"*I'*m really bad," Todd told me. "I was named after my father—'the big jerk.' That's what my mother called him."

Todd Sr. had left the family shortly after Todd was born. Todd's mother, Kate, quickly became involved with Roger, a man with a short temper and a strong love for beer. Two years after Todd was born, Kate had a baby girl, June. Roger paid the rent, bought the food, and paid the bills. He also spanked Todd—hard—for every infraction he could find. Kate just looked the other way. By the time Todd was 4, he wanted desperately to hit Roger back. But he didn't dare. He knew he'd be killed. Instead, Todd would beg for attention from his mother. He'd whine and plead for snacks, for sweets, and for help.

---

* © 1974 by Evil Eye Music, Inc. Reprinted by permission.

"Get it yourself," Kate would scold. "What's the matter with you? Can't you see I'm busy? Look at this mess your sister made!"

Todd simmered. Then he'd "accidentally" knock over a dish, a lamp, or forget to close the door, and the cat would run out. Kate yelled at him, louder and harder, with an edge in her voice. That's when Todd started to hate everyone, even his mother. He walked around in a rage, cursing under his breath, spitting out the same words that Roger used to yell at him.

By the time he got to kindergarten, Todd moved like a miniature cyclone: Looking left, right, and rarely at his work, bumping into every child in the class, and always ready to fight. When another child was upset, Todd was right there repeating the words he knew so well, words that bit and tore at your heart: "You're an idiot! You'll never win! Jackass! Asshole!" Then came the inevitable fight, and Todd moved into his glory.

By October, Todd was well known to the principal. By November, he was in a special class. By the time he was in fourth grade, the school had had enough and urged Kate to file a petition in court citing Todd as a PINS. The principal wanted Todd placed in a special school.

Kate agreed. "I'm sick of his attitude!" she told the principal. She went to the courthouse, filled out an application form, and petitioned the court to manage Todd because he was incorrigible, defiant, and aggressive to her, to peers, and to teachers.

Seated before the judge, Todd felt an ache deep inside. He knew he must be really bad—a criminal about to be sentenced. His mother was right. He was no good. "You're just like your father," Kate had told him. "You're never going to amount to anything."

The judge listened intently as the petition citing Todd's trans-
gressions and disobedience was read. Todd watched the court
stenographer record each word: "Defiant. Incorrigible." He didn't
even understand some of the words, but he knew what they
meant. He was bad, really bad.

The judge scowled and ordered Todd to learn to behave.
By court order, Todd was sent to a residential treatment center
90 miles away from his mother's home for 18 months.

Todd was heartbroken but resigned. He tried to do his best
at the residential treatment center. He learned the rules; he earned
points for good behavior. Week after week, he'd call his mother
and beg her to take him home.

"Let me see what your social workers say," Kate would reply.
She never called Todd and often was too busy to talk to him
when he called her.

"I've got to fix dinner for Roger and June. Gotta go. Be
good!" she said sternly. Then her voice softened. "I'll see you, soon
as I can." Todd could imagine the smile he missed so much and
the twinkle in his mother's eyes when her voice lilted up.

But Kate rarely visited. Sometimes she just didn't show up.
Other times, she called minutes before their appointment. "The
car broke down," she'd tell the treatment center staff. "June is
sick," or "I'm not feeling well—I just can't shake this flu."

Todd would hear his mother's message from his social worker
and storm out of the office. Minutes later he'd get into a fight,
hitting, kicking, and cursing.

When his mother did show up at the residential treatment
center, Todd drew colorful pictures of himself holding out flow-
ers for her, red roses for Mother's Day, tulips for Easter, a bou-

quet for Christmas. The social worker tried to get Todd to talk to his mother, to share his successes, his goals, and his feelings. Todd couldn't look his mother in the eye. He would lower his head and mumble as his mother looked down on him. "I'm doing better... I got all my points in school."

Kate would turn to the social worker. "Is he still bold? Has he showed you how bad he can be?" Kate would nod when she heard about his fighting with other kids. Then she'd tell Todd to shape up if he wanted to come home.

"We're trying to build up his skills. He could be great in sports, but he won't even try," staff told Kate. Todd refused to play sports. He said he was no good. Instead, he'd take apart radios and tape recorders, examine the pieces, and leave them sprawled over his room. Todd would inspect the parts when he got back to his room. If anyone touched his things, Todd would shriek.

Weeks and months went by. Todd worked hard at school and pulled himself up to grade level. He proudly showed his mother his report card at a meeting to review his progress.

Todd asked about June. "I really miss her," he told his mother.

"You'll see her soon," Kate promised.

"What about Roger? Would he come to one of our meetings?" Todd's social worker asked Kate.

"I'd like to see him," Todd interjected, still looking down.

"You'll see him when you come home," Kate replied.

Kate never mentioned the drugs or alcoholic binges every weekend, the beatings Todd had endured from Roger, or how she was rarely home. But what hurt the most were her comments to Todd's social worker and child care staff. She'd smile at the staff like they were her best friends and sigh, "He's been this way since the day he was born. I just can't handle him. The school kicked him out, the principal hates him—they don't want him. He's like his father. I knew he'd never amount to anything. He's just no good!"

Todd kept his head down, his eyes lowered. Inside, he was boiling, but he wouldn't show it. He wanted to bite his mother's head off, but he couldn't even open his mouth. One word, and he knew she could destroy him.

"I'll never come back," Kate had warned him. Todd was terrified that he would lose his mother, his sister, everybody he knew, forever. If he spoke out against his mother, she might never let him come home.

The Curse

I met Todd after he finished two years in the residential treatment center. He was 12 years old and still classified as a PINS, an "incorrigible" youth. Todd had improved enough in his behaviors to get out of the residential treatment facility. Tall and scrawny with a gentle curve to his cheeks, Todd hardly looked like the hardened delinquent described in his mother's court petitions.

"I don't believe he's really changed," his mother told her social worker. "I can't take a chance, for June's sake. I just can't deal right now with the way Todd acts. Not if he gets violent again." She refused to take Todd home for a visit. "He can come home when I know he's really changed. When I know he can act right, and not be so bold!"

Todd was referred to my agency's foster family program to help him learn the skills he would need to resume living in a family. In our program, Kate was asked to work hard to help Todd return home. Since Todd was now living near her home, she knew that the old excuses wouldn't work. Kate was reminded that the state law allowed a parent a year to work to make things better before a decision needed to be made about where the child would grow up permanently. Todd had already been placed away from home for two and a half years. He needed to know if she could raise him. She needed to make a choice as a parent, as the adult.

Kate complained that Roger was in the way, causing problems. After one weekend of drinking and fighting, she kicked him out. A month later, Kate decided that she couldn't handle her daughter June.

"She's following in Todd's footsteps," Kate declared. She filed a PINS petition in family court. June was sent to the same residential treatment center that had worked with Todd.

Pressed to help her children, Kate said she was exhausted and overwhelmed. She missed appointments and showed up weeks later with Ed, her new boyfriend. Kate pulled Todd aside in one visit. "I can't take you home, not just now. Ed doesn't want any kids."

Six months later, Kate gave birth to a baby boy. Two months afterward, she met with the judge and signed papers surrendering her legal rights to Todd.

Kate told Roger he could have June. She visited Todd to say goodbye and to tell him that she couldn't handle him or June. She was making a new life. Two days later, Todd threatened to punch out a younger boy in his foster family. His foster parents tried to talk to him, but he slammed the door in their faces and threatened them as well. After a week of defiance, Todd was asked to leave their home.

Todd settled in well with his new foster family and his second foster mother, Betty. He liked Betty's home in the city. He liked his new teacher. But two months later, Betty complained that Todd kept badgering the other children in her foster home, making cutting remarks, and getting into other people's business. He never seemed to stop.

"Todd could be good," said Betty. "He seems to want to help." But he kept pushing the other kids, first with words, and then, if Betty or her husband didn't intervene, he'd start slugging. It was getting to be too much, Betty said to Todd's social worker. "He's got to change or leave. He's just too annoying, aggravating, and hurtful. He disrupts the other kids."

Todd shared with me a picture of how his previous foster parents had made him "blow his top." He pictured his head flying off to the side of himself, with a deep frown on his face. "This is how I felt when they made fun of me!" Todd wrote. Dark lines moved outward from his head to the left and right, and a small dark cloud hung above. An arrow connected the head on his body with the head blown off to the side. In the middle, he shaded in dark clouds filled with streaks. The figure had well-defined hands and large shoulders, but no feet to stand on.

I was struck with the energy Todd's foster parents' words triggered in him. Todd clearly carried power within him. I wondered how we could rechannel that power. I looked for the message in Todd's aggravating behavior. He was about to get Betty to kick him out of her family and thus confirm, once again in his mind, how bad he was. At the same time, Todd was still drawing pictures for me of his mother and himself together. He pictured his mother with large hands and a wide smile looking ahead while a second head on her shoulder gazed toward Todd with the caption "I love you, kiss." Todd drew himself standing next to his mother with elongated fingers and a wide, brightly colored smile as he answered his mother, "I love you too, Mom."

I thought of Todd's mother as the two-headed monster in that picture, beguiling the world with her charm and smile while she gave her son a perfunctory kiss with her other self. It was a show. I angrily visualized Kate's sweet double messages, visit after visit, and felt my fingers stretch out—did Todd also feel an urge to throttle his mother? I felt equally angered at the years Todd had been labeled as a delinquent by authorities and at the pressure the court and residential center had placed on this boy to change on his own, while his mother did nothing to help heal the troubles she had helped to create. Her messages of love covered the poison in her repeated attacks.

I also knew that Todd loved his mother. He had sketched a picture of the mother he wished for. No one can give up all they have yearned for when there is nothing to take its place. But holding this love also meant holding on to the messages Kate had repeated over and over throughout Todd's lifetime: "You're no good! You'll never amount to anything!" And the worst message of all: "Get out!"

This was the curse Todd held inside. The belief that he was no good had grown along with Todd, year by year, hammered inside him with every rejection by his mother. The curse had become deeply embedded within the very marrow of his bones. The harsh words and biting tone of his mother's voice hit Todd like an icy blast of wind, and with Kate's sudden decision to surrender her rights, the curse swirled faster and harder, like a winter storm blowing in Todd's mind.

Todd's body and mind exploded. Hitting, kicking, and cursing, Todd enacted his unspoken rage at his mother's abandonment. With every blow and obscenity, Todd gave life to the curse and offered up another reason for everyone in his world to hate him, to punish him, and to once again abandon him.

Teamwork

I knew that Todd could never face the curse without people at his side he cared about and who cared about him. I worried that Betty was becoming too caught up in trying to battle Todd and that her ultimatums would only reinforce his belief that she would soon kick him out like everyone else. At our review meetings, I tried to coach Betty to try a different approach and rise above Todd's provocations.

Betty held firm in her home. I admired her courage and her convictions. She matched Todd's hard-headedness with her own stubborn and feisty spirit, reinforced by her husband, her children, her church, and her large extended family. She weathered Todd's provocations and kept him in line with the power of her voice, and best of all, Betty kept him week after week.

"I'd like to see my grandfather. But I really want to see my sister," Todd told me. He worried about her. He missed her. Todd wanted to help her and to apologize for picking on her. June's father, Roger, didn't want any contact with Todd. He had never apologized for his abuse of Todd and instead, recited his memories of how Todd had defied him and provoked June. With perseverance, Mary, Todd's new social worker, convinced Roger to allow Todd to visit with his half-sister on a trial basis.

Todd transformed into the quintessential big brother when he saw June. He coached her on what to do and say to get out of the residential center. He apologized for hitting her in their fights. Together, they remembered stories of the good times they had.

Todd shared with me a picture of a heart and a smiling face that he drew to represent himself with his sister. We talked about the power of Todd and June, brother and sister. Todd looked at his picture and paused. "Happiness and love keep us alive," he said.

No one had been able to locate Todd's father or paternal relatives, but Mary finally found Todd's maternal grandfather and set up a visit. Grandpa Phil was dying from cancer when Mary located him, but he welcomed a chance to see his grandson. Todd was very nervous about visiting his grandfather, but he warmed up when Grandpa Phil reached out to him. "I know you love your mother, but I've known her all her life," Phil told him. "Todd, you're a good boy. You just can't trust your mother."

A few weeks after Todd's visit, Grandpa Phil died. Later, when I saw Todd, he remembered his grandfather's last words to him. "She shouldn't have sent you away, Todd. Just don't believe her." I almost sighed out loud. Grandpa Phil's words gave Todd an antidote to the curse.

Thanks to Mary's efforts, Todd had regained his sister as an ally and had reconnected to his grandfather. Once a boy on his own with nothing but a yearning for his mother, Todd now had a team: his foster mother, Betty; his social worker, Mary; his sister, June; and the memory of Grandpa Phil. It was time to go to war against the curse.

The Battle

I met with Todd to help develop his sense of safety and skills in relaxing himself and then to help him overcome the snag that kept him always on the brink of being rejected again. We call it trauma therapy, and the first steps involve building up enough trust and security so that a child can begin to approach their worst nightmares. Todd brought up recent incidents in which his child care worker, Fran, had reprimanded him. Fran took the children in Betty's foster family to activities, managed the household every Thursday night, and served as a mentor for Todd and the other children.

Todd's stomach felt "delicate" as he remembered being scolded. Todd could also see himself in a positive way as "lovable, smart, and kind." But Todd had trouble shaking the image in his mind of Fran yelling at him to be to quiet. The scold in her voice pierced through his bravado and once again confirmed how bad he was. "I'm too loud," he said.

Nothing seemed to help until I brought up one of his favorite cartoon characters, a lovable dog with long floppy ears. For a moment, we imagined that Fran had become this dog, and Todd visualized this dog and himself together in the kitchen of his foster family's home. Todd grinned as he ended his story: "I gave her a hug and she hugged me back."

Todd's body swayed slightly as if he was actually embracing Fran, and I could almost feel how much Todd craved the warmth of a hug. "Okay. I'd like to go now," Todd said, standing up.

Two weeks later, I waited for Todd to show up for our next appointment. Instead, Betty stopped by to tell me that Todd was even more agitated than usual. He was wandering about the building, refusing to talk to anyone. She left to look for him. A few minutes later, Todd strode into my office, his head tilted down with a deeply set frown.

"I'm AWOL!" Todd declared, pacing back and forth in my office.

"What's going on?" I asked, inviting Todd to sit with me. Todd continued to pace and made jabbing motions with his arms. "Fran hates me. She yelled at me. I'm sick of it! She won't let me go to my room. I can't take a break! You tell me to take a break. She won't let me! I can't even get away!"

"What do you think would help?"

Todd kept pacing, a difficult feat given the size of my office. Every time he approached the door or a wall, he wrenched himself into a turn and headed back again, creating a jerking sense of motion, back and forth, back and forth, with no relief.

I pulled out a foam boomerang I had recently purchased. I showed the boomerang to Todd and asked him if he could get it to work. Todd picked it up and hurled it hard. The boomerang crashed downward in a spiral. Todd tried several more times, gradually decreasing the force of his throw until the boomerang actually started to curve.

"That's the best throw I've seen," I said and then confided. "I can't get it to come back at all." I could appreciate Todd's skill with a toy that frustrated me.

"I want to go to my room. Just be by myself." Todd declared. I could see he was about to launch into another series of diatribes about his child care worker. Just then, Betty knocked on the door, and I invited her to sit down and join us. Todd stopped his pacing but remained standing.

"I tell him, 'This is not your mother's house.'" Betty said. This usually worked to interrupt Todd's rage a little, but sometimes she couldn't get to Todd soon enough. Betty wanted Todd to act his age and learn to manage himself without leaving a situation. I noticed Todd listening carefully, his mouth set into a deep frown. With Betty and I sitting, Todd looked down at us.

"Why do you keep bringing up the past?" Todd countered, looking at me and ignoring his foster mother.

"Because you keep doing the old stuff," I responded. "Would you like to get past the old stuff?"

Todd turned his head away. I could see his hands squeeze into the back of a chair harder and harder, then release.

"All right," Todd grunted.

We talked about giving Todd a chance to do something different. I encouraged Todd to practice a simple response when he felt people were putting him down. He could stop himself and touch symbols he could carry in his pocket from Betty; Mary, a former child care worker he had liked; and the minister of his church. Touching these special mementos would remind him of people who cared and help interrupt his usual cycle of escalating anger. I invited Todd to practice imagining that the person who was annoying him had transformed into one of his favorite cartoon characters. Instead of sliding into his standard angry and violent response, Todd could assertively ask to take a break to calm himself, just as he had requested. Fran and Betty agreed to let Todd go off by himself when he asked appropriately.

Winning on the Court

At our next meeting, I began by asking Todd to tell me about some of his good memories. Todd remembered a former child care worker who had taken him out for a special present and how Todd knew she loved him because she did special things for him.

"How do you feel about yourself when you are with her?" I asked Todd.

"I have a lot of respect," Todd answered. He liked the feeling, but he often felt just the opposite. For instance, Todd shared how kids in his gym class had teased him recently for being no good at sports. As Todd thought about this image, he saw himself as "no good." He wanted to believe that he was good, but he couldn't. Todd sketched a picture of himself with the other kids in the gym class playing volleyball, and he said he felt nervous. I asked him to imagine himself looking at the scene on the volleyball court as though he was watching from the upper deck of a stadium, peering through binoculars.

"My stomach hurts," Todd shared.

I saw the pain in Todd's face, but at the same time, I was reassured. Todd was hurting terribly inside, but not so much that he had turned off all feeling. Todd had shared stories with me about how he helped other youth. He certainly tormented other kids with taunts and challenges, but often came back later and apologized. Despite all the years he lived with abuse and neglect, Todd retained the capacity to care. He also reminded us that he needed a family of his own.

I asked Todd to add his favorite cartoon character to the volleyball court. Todd enacted his dog-friend ordering the other kids, "Leave him alone." Todd continued on with his story and visualized himself saying these words louder and louder to the other kids.

"I'm feeling okay now," Todd said at the end of his story. He imagined his peers becoming his friends.

The Battle

A few weeks later, Todd drew a picture of June with a large smiling face, and he remembered his little sister's smile when he had bought her a cookie, one day long ago. He had used the money he earned from returning soda bottles to the store. Todd looked at his sister's picture and thought she was "beautiful, nice, and friendly."

Betty reported that Todd was doing better in her home. Betty would give Todd a hug and tuck him firmly into bed every night. Despite his size, Todd was still a little boy inside, wishing for someone to hold him and give him a kiss goodnight.

Every three or four days, however, his frustration would rise, and Todd would be at the epicenter of another altercation. Todd told Mary how his mother had yelled at him that he was no good and would never amount to anything.

"I'm really bad...I'm no good," Todd repeated over and over to himself. As he said the words, his fists clenched, and his face hardened. That's when he'd start teasing other kids, trying to get them angry.

I imagined Kate's words striking Todd like a poison dart, but Todd also remembered how she'd fixed him breakfast in the morning and kissed him on the forehead. We talked about Todd pulling out the poison dart, the courage he had had to show to get this far, and what he could do to earn the privileges of a 12-year-old.

"Who believes you can't do it?" I challenged Todd. "Betty? June? Mary? Fran?"

Todd grabbed a piece of paper and scribbled, "I love you."

I watched as Todd intently wrote these words over and over, a hundred times.

"That's for my mom!" Todd said firmly.

My heart sank. I feared he would never let go of his longing for Kate to care for him.

He looked up at me. "I mean *Betty*," Todd continued, his voice getting deeper and stronger as he spoke. "She said I could stay as long as I wanted."

Todd took another sheet of paper and sketched a swirling vortex. With dark lines, he drew Kate standing at the bottom of a cliff holding a rope. His mother grinned with teeth on one side of her mouth and a small dark cloud over her head. The rope spiraled upward and was lashed to Todd's waist. Todd pictured himself looking down at his mother from the edge of the cliff, a quivering smile on his face.

"What's going to happen?" I asked.

Todd etched his mother's words in block letters. "I've got you," she said.

Todd added his sister to the drawing, standing next to him—brother and sister, side by side, holding hands.

Todd pictured himself replying, "I do not think so. You'll never get us! You wicked curser!"

I smiled. I could hear the strength in Todd's voice. I wanted him to remember this image, his courage, his victory.

"What music would be playing?" I asked, inviting Todd to make the story into an Academy Award-winning movie. In my mind, I expected Todd to pick a rock and roll or rap artist with booming voice. I thought of Tom Petty's "I *won't* back down" or the Grateful Dead singing "I *will* get by." I assumed Todd would pick a male vocalist, a song of triumph.

Todd sat back, like a movie director pondering from his chair, and then leaned forward, a smile on his face. "You can count on me through thick and thin...Whitney Houston."

Letting Go

Todd was approaching the one-year anniversary of moving into Betty's home. "I never stayed in any home that long," Todd thought out loud.

"Todd is still agitating other children in the home," Betty said. "Much less so now, but he can't seem to hold back when he sees another child upset. I tell him, 'Let it go.'"

Betty, Mary and I talked about how to develop a ceremony to mark this occasion and also how to honor Todd's new relationship with Betty's family.

"They said I could call them 'Mom' and 'Dad,'" Todd told me later. He sketched a picture of a heart. "It means they will always be there," Todd told me.

I pulled out Todd's drawing of his battle against Kate's curse, and we explored different ways Todd could break the curse, imagining June by his side and bringing in Betty's voice, "Let it go."

"I dreamt of an angel last night," Todd told me.

"What do you think it meant?" I asked.

"God and the angel are with me," Todd answered.

The next time I saw Todd, he drew a symbol for me of the power of his sister and himself together. I asked Todd to draw the curse the way it was when he was living in the residential program, three years earlier. He sketched a huge tangled blob that looked like a tornado swirling through space.

"That's when I was forgotten."

"How does it look now?" I asked.

Todd drew a heart around the swirl. "The heart is holding in the curse," Todd said. He told me that he felt wanted and lovable in Betty's home, the opposite of how he had felt when he was sent by his mother and the judge to the residential program.

"What fed the curse?" I asked Todd.

"My mom kept June. She kept her drinking and drugs a secret. Then she sent June away but kept Eddie, her new boyfriend's baby. And she blamed me and June. She said I would never amount to anything, just like my father. And she lied. She told me she couldn't come to visit me when the county gave her the money. She told June not to visit me."

We talked about ways Todd could take away even more of the power of the curse by shattering the secrets and the lies.

Beating the Curse

Time after time, Todd reminded me that it was his link to his little sister and the love he felt from Betty, her husband, and their family that gave him the courage he needed to defeat the curse. He wanted to show June, "You can count on me," the theme of his favorite song. Todd and June together, beating the curse.

Like most people, I could only begin to imagine how hard it was for Todd to face a mother who had branded him as no good, approved of his stepfather hitting him, and then confirmed his shame by sending him away from home, blaming him for her problems, and using his rebellion as a justification for keeping him away. I never experienced the rejection and abandonment that Todd felt growing up, but I could feel the sting of his mother's words and how her curse had cut Todd apart.

Mary persevered in her efforts to get Kate to meet with Todd and acknowledge her responsibility for placing Todd and his sister. Kate canceled sessions, would simply not show up, or would not be home when Mary drove out to her house. But finally, she agreed to come in to see Todd.

With Mary's help, Todd mustered the courage to ask his mother the question that had been burning for so many years in his heart. "If you really loved me, why did you give me up?"

"My drugs got in the way," Kate replied. "It was too hard to visit. I knew I couldn't do what I had to do to get you or your sister back. So I signed the surrender. You deserved a good family," Kate told Todd.

Kate eventually began allowing Todd to see Eddie for brief visits and, again, with Mary's perseverance, he was occasionally able to meet with June. Despite her verbalized validation of Todd, Kate periodically wrote messages to Todd blaming him for his years of placement and complaining of how hard life had been to her. Each message tore at Todd's fragile sense of self and he would typically provoke another child or his foster parents to become enraged with him. Still, with the support and caring of Betty and her family, Todd adjusted to his new home. Within two years of his placement in Betty's home, he made it to the honor roll in his school, and four years later, he graduated from high school.

I thought of a prominent congressional leader who had been calling for America to rebuild its orphanages to care for the half a million children who need to live apart from their birthfamilies. I wished he could have met Todd, heard Todd's story, and seen how Todd looked at Betty. Todd showed me that every child needs a family who loves him or her. But much more than that, Todd showed me how a heart can wrap around a tornado—how a boy can break a curse if he has the help of a family he can count on.

In popular movies and video games, warriors battle by themselves, and fighting is both a means of survival and a source of power. But in the real world of Todd's life, macho images of tough young men battling alone against bad guys just didn't work. Todd showed me that real strength comes with the courage to fight for people you care about. I admired his courage to keep looking for a family, even when state authorities pressed him to accept a goal of independent living. It would have been much easier for Todd to give up on anybody ever caring for him and to curse the world for all the years of neglect he had experienced.

To let go of the curse, Todd needed family members he could hold on to. Grandpa Phil gave Todd a new way to look at himself and his mother. June brought out the part of Todd that could become a hero, strong enough to battle his mother's words. Betty and her husband saw the good side of this "bad" boy and gave Todd a second chance at growing up with hugs, chores, and a family he could call his own, with siblings, aunts, uncles, and cousins. Betty's church welcomed Todd into their community, giving him a place to feel like a normal youth taking part in services and youth group activities.

"Look Around"

Snow fell softly on the narrow city streets. It was dark and the driving was slippery. I pulled up to the old brick church and was struck by the number of cars on this snowy evening. Betty's invitation card had said simply, "Join us in celebrating."

Inside, Mary welcomed the guests followed by a prayer from the minister. Mary's daughter sang a song, and a family friend read a prayer written by Todd thanking his new family, his minister, and his friends. The congregation sang Todd's favorite hymn. Then, Mary presented Todd with a certificate to help him always remember this ceremony and how Todd had become a permanent member of Betty's family.

Betty stepped forward. One by one, she introduced her grown children.

"This is Steve. Todd, he is your family now."

"This is Rachel. Todd, she is your family now."

"This is Benjamin. Todd, he is your family now."

Then, she introduced her children's spouses and her children's children.

"We are all here for you, Todd. Whenever you need anyone, look around." Betty paused, then looked directly at Todd. "Now you have a family that is yours."

13
BRENDA

In the middle of difficulty lies opportunity.

–Albert Einstein

*B*renda's grades had jumped from 60s in social studies to a 96. She had cut back her fighting with peers and was looking forward to being adopted. I asked her to picture herself. Brenda sketched a ray of light.

Brenda described how she had "gotten used to" the abuse and neglect of her birthfamily. She had been labeled a delinquent for her stealing and fighting. Only after moving into Lisa and Jim's home was she able to disclose her father's sexual abuse, her stepfather's drunken violence and flirtation, and her mother's demands that Brenda keep quiet and help her mother care for her new baby sister.

"I can't change it," Brenda said, referring to the violence and abuse of the past. But she felt she could become like the ray of light, spreading everywhere, and touching people in a warm way.

"What powers the ray of light?" I asked.

"Lisa and Jim," Brenda said, indicating her preadoptive foster parents. "They're my heroes."

"...And myself," she added.

Traumatized children look for special moments to share the secrets of their lives with people who will protect them. When family members and caring adults take action, the walls surrounding children crumble and the angels are no longer hidden. These are the magic moments that reveal the power of caring.

RANDY

There is no such thing as a baby;
there is a baby and someone.

–D.W. Winnicott

*R*andy started life with chemical abuse in utero and physical abuse as a boy. Marge, his mother, remembered yelling, "Stop that!" when Randy began kicking inside her belly. Randy was born with a light, almost white complexion, but Marge knew her Irish Catholic family would see his curly hair and resent her, even more than before, for taking up with a black man, a man who had left her soon after she became pregnant. She was alone when Randy was born. Alcohol and cocaine were her best friends. Marge resolved to do it on her own.

As an infant, Randy would lie so still that Marge feared he had died. She even pricked him with a pin to make sure he was alive. When he developed a seizure disorder, failed to talk, and balked at toilet training, Marge knew she didn't want this baby.

139

She convinced her mother to take him into her home while she
entered a rehab facility. Even after stopping the drugs and alcohol, she just never quite got herself together enough to ask for
Randy back. Months passed, Marge moved in and out of relationships, slipped back twice into an alcoholic haze, but somehow
managed to pull herself back each time and start again. Then
Marge's father had a stroke, and her mother told her she could
no longer care for Randy. Randy was 4 years old. Despite speech
and language therapy and a special education preschool, he was
still markedly delayed in every area. Once again, Marge resolved
to do it on her own.

Marge held herself together for two years, but she slipped
again back into drinking after a boyfriend left her. Randy was
difficult for her. He made a mess of the apartment, whined a lot,
and cried when she came near him.

One day, Marge just lost it. Randy had left crumbs and food
all over the kitchen table, counters, and floor. She started to yell.
Randy knocked plates and glasses off the table. It was Marge's
breaking point. Marge grabbed a plastic bat lying near by and
smacked Randy on the back. Two days later, with CPS workers at
her door, Marge called her aunt and begged her to take Randy.

In his great-aunt's home, Randy tagged along after his older
cousin Matthew. Matthew taught Randy to shoot baskets and
play football. Randy became a good shot. He was only fair at
dribbling, but his height helped him win games. He was sought
after by boys in his aunt's neighborhood and began to make
friends. Randy adored his cousin and managed to spend most of
the next four years at his great-aunt's house. Marge began taking
him weekdays, but on weekends, Randy begged to visit his cousin
at his great-aunt's home.

When Randy turned 10, Matthew headed off for college and Randy's great-aunt decided to move to Arizona. Marge and Randy were on their own once again.

Within a year, Marge had begun drinking again. Once, Randy made a mess of the house. Marge yelled at him, and Randy shuddered and pulled back. Marge looked down and saw her son, a coward, something she could never tolerate in her own life, something she had fought against from her earliest days. For Marge, cowardice meant weakness. Her rage intensified, and Marge smacked Randy with a broom, cursed at him for being so stupid, and left him with a large enough bruise to bring in CPS. Randy was placed into an emergency foster home.

When Randy first came to our crisis center, he was threatening to kill himself. He would punch himself on the leg and jaw. When upset, he'd wander off and get lost, forgetting how he got where he was. Randy responded to insults from peers with a sense of being attacked by the world. When adults yelled at him, reality and memories merged. He'd simmer for a time, trying to close himself off from the fast words his assailants hurled at him. But the words pricked like a thousand stings. Inside, Randy felt a panic rise up. His eyes narrowed. He would try to look away, but he was drawn back. He felt his arms tense and his back stiffen.

Randy would bark at the youth or adult he perceived to be his chief tormentor, "Stop it!" "Don't!" "I'm warning you!" But it only took one more word, one more barb, from anyone. Randy would attack anyone and everyone in his way. Randy was wiry, but by early adolescence, he towered over his classmates and many teachers. Impulsive and easily provoked, Randy became known as a threat, a youth to watch out for. But Randy was also an easy target for other students—someone you could get riled up on a boring day in class, someone you could always count on for a good show. Fights in the cafeteria led to suspensions. Suspensions led to expulsions, and expulsions led to special schools. Each detention, each suspension, hit Randy like another slap from his mother, a confirmation of how stupid he was, how unwanted.

"Punk"

When I met Randy, he had been diagnosed with mild mental retardation, expressive and receptive language delays, and fetal alcohol and cocaine syndrome. Therapists described him as oppositionally defiant, suicidal, aggressive, and suffering from post-traumatic stress disorder. Randy's long history of severe behavior problems, school suspensions, and multiple placements pointed toward a life in long-term detention.

"I gotta hurry up and do something," Randy told me when I met him alone the first time. He was 14 years old. "Put me in a group home, or something!" Randy had gotten into fights at school almost every day in the last month. The fights had started after his mother changed her mind and decided that she wanted Randy to return from family foster care to her home. The worst fights took place on Tuesdays, just before his weekly visit with his mother.

Kids would taunt Randy, calling him "stupid" and "punk." That was all it took; Randy had to show he was not afraid. He had learned his mother's lesson.

Randy was instructed by teachers to calm down, think of something else, and try to talk it out. But Randy couldn't slow himself down. He just simmered until he blew up. Randy just wanted to run away and never come back. "I feel like hitting the teachers, but I don't want to do that—I won't do it!"

Randy slowly sketched a picture for me of his mother rising above him. Both of them wore sunglasses and their hands were hidden behind their backs. "What's happening?" I asked.

"I'm going to stay with my mother," he replied.

Randy was known as a terror in school, but seated at a table with his mother, Randy kept his head down, rarely looking up— and he never looked directly at his mother.

"My walls are up!" Marge said, starting our family meeting. "How come you have to get into so much trouble?" she demanded, staring forcefully at Randy. "And how come you don't *talk* to me?"

Marge described how she was taking one day at a time, working her 12-step program. I asked about hitting, since Randy was showing us one fight after another. Marge candidly shared how she had beaten Randy with a belt for everything he did wrong when he lived with her. She beat him if he couldn't remember the alphabet. She beat him if he couldn't defend himself against other boys. Marge called him "stupid" and "punk," the same words that triggered his attacks on peers at school.

"This isn't working," Marge stated with an edge in her voice, referring to therapy. "Randy hasn't got time for this *bullshit* and neither do *I*."

Randy had never shared his anger to his mother for her beatings and emotional abuse. When we were alone, Randy told me that he was afraid, afraid of his mother hitting him again, afraid that he would hit her back and never stop. At school, the teachers pulled him off other kids and kept everyone safe. At home, it was just Randy and Marge.

In our family session, we talked about Marge's options: to continue working to reunite with her son or to make a plan for

Randy to grow up in another family, though hopefully with continuing contact with Marge.

"I've decided to drop my custody petition," Marge said bluntly. I looked up in surprise. Marge looked at the door. "That's it! Are we done here?"

But Randy was far from being done. He continued to visit his mother and to wish that she would take him home. He ran from his foster family, got lost, and was brought back by the police. When confronted at school, Randy threatened to jump off a bridge. Then he forced his way out of the building and headed toward the river.

Randy was brought back once again to his foster family, but they had had enough. Two weeks later, Randy was suspended again from school. His social worker needed to find him another foster family.

Randy had initially hoped to live with his grandparents, but he knew that wouldn't work. Then he wanted to live with his great-aunt. Randy's social worker tried for months to contact her and invited her to attend meetings when she was in the area on visits. She did write him a letter, which said that Randy's cousin was doing well in college and told Randy to stay out of trouble. "Promise you'll stay in school," his great-aunt wrote. Randy kept asking to see her, to visit her, to talk to her, but she never quite made the meetings that were set up. I encouraged Randy to ask her directly for a visit. After several months, Randy realized she would not take him.

"Everybody forgot me," Randy told me, as he thought about his family. "I want to keep seeing my mother. I will never make it on my own."

A New Home

"I tell all my kids, 'This is my home,'" said Sandy, Randy's new foster mother, at our next planning meeting for Randy. "No matter what you do, we will work it out. I won't let you go." Randy grinned his sneaky grin and stared at the floor.

"What are you thinking?" I asked.

"Nothing," Randy replied and smiled even more. "Just how Sandy keeps telling me, 'Clean your room. Clean your room. Clean your room.' But she's just as bad as me!" Randy had a contagious grin. Sandy smiled back and repeated the rules of her home.

Randy started a prevocational training program in the afternoons and developed an interest in gardening. He liked plants, and he was amazingly gentle with his hands. Randy also liked a class in cooking; Southern fried chicken was his favorite. He especially admired an African American culinary arts teacher. Randy's grades changed from Fs to Cs in his special education classes.

Sandy and her husband, Paul, started bringing both Irish American and African American customs into their home. At our family meetings, Sandy invited Marge to share her traditions and special memories about Randy and her family. Marge only came to half the meetings, but she told Randy he could be honest with her and tell her how he felt. Randy, however, continued to keep his head down, his eyes glued to the floor. With his mother present, he could only stammer.

Saying the Words

Randy was now 15 years old and the size of a man—a tall, handsome man. He stood out, rugged looking, one of only a few youth of mixed race in his high school. Girls in his high school flirted with Randy. Boys admired his size and strength. He loved the attention. Randy became excited. He suddenly felt proud, but the flattery often turned into rejections and teasing. Flirtatious smiles changed into taunts. Boasts turned into challenges and fights. He was still an easy target for youth looking for someone to push into a fight with a few taunts. A slap and a poke and Randy would fly off, a warrior in motion. With one shove, Randy would knock the other youth down. He would press the other youth to the floor with his knee and pin the youth's arms above his head. Randy taught his tormentors how it felt to be helpless.

Teachers would run in, pull Randy off his tormentor, and march him into the principal's office, who would send him back to his foster family, suspended once again. Randy was still on the edge, still seen as a danger, still lashing out at anyone who reminded him of the barbs he carried inside.

"I'm afraid I'm going to hit a girl," Randy told me. He fantasized about putting a boy he knew in a headlock, choking him, and killing another youth. But he also thought about the police coming to get him, going to jail, getting into fights in jail. "I might as well kill myself right here and now," he said.

Randy felt the rage boiling inside him. Still afraid to talk to his mother, Randy carried the memories of her beatings and her taunts. He still felt every place on his body where she had hit him. Her rebukes and ridicule still reverberated in his mind. These were scars Randy carried from the past.

Randy told me he wanted to tell his mother, "I can't forgive you for hitting me," but he was afraid she would snap at him. "If she got mad, I don't know what I'd do. I might hit her. Nothing could keep me safe!" he said. The more Randy thought about his mother, the more afraid he became that he might someday end up beating a girlfriend or a wife. Randy told me that he didn't want to hit his own partner or kids.

A few weeks later, Randy's mother called and asked him if he wanted to live with her. He told her to wait until they had some visits. Randy looked older to me then than I had remembered. The smirky smile was gone. His voice was soft but surprising strong.

"What could you do if she got angry during a visit?" I asked.

"I think all she'd do now is holler," said Randy. "I could just tell her to calm down. Go to her room. Just tell me what I need to do, clean my room, clean the dishes, whatever."

"What would you tell your mom about the hitting?" I asked.

"I was just hurt by it. I don't want to hit my kids!" Randy recognized that he couldn't go back to live with his mother. "I just want be able to see my family. I don't want to lose them."

A month later, however, Randy was talking about going back to live in his mother's home.

"I want to see my aunt and my cousin. It's my fault I'm in foster care. I want to be with my mom. What if she gets sick again? I want to be there when she gets sick, so I can help her." Marge had gotten sick with pneumonia recently.

I challenged Randy to summon the courage to tell his mother about his fears and his wish to care for her when she got sick. We talked about ways to keep himself calm, people who he could bring with him, ways to show how he felt and still show respect.

Marge came to our planning meeting and told Randy he needed to grow up. I urged Marge to show Randy how she had changed by coming to family sessions and spending time with Randy, by demonstrating that they could talk and stay safe from the hitting and the anger they both carried inside. I tried to put into words the unspoken fears Randy hid from his mother and hoped she could help him understand where her own pain and impulsive anger came from, long before his birth. I urged Marge to convince Randy that she could hear his true feelings without losing control of her own temper, hitting him, or worse, hurting herself by going back to the drugs and alcohol and abandoning Randy once again by discontinuing her visits. Could he stay in his foster family and not have to worry that she had gotten terribly ill again without his knowing? Would she or another relative let Randy know if she got sick again?

Marge asked Randy to be honest with her. She promised to keep in touch and to let Randy or his foster mother know if she ever got sick again. It was a start.

A Second Chance

As it turned out, it was not Marge, but Randy who needed medical help. It happened during a visit to his mother's home. Randy was reaching for a top shelf, standing on a rickety chair when he toppled, falling with his ankle twisted. Marge rushed him to the hospital, where they learned that Randy's ankle was fractured and that he would need to be in a cast for several weeks. Marge stayed with Randy in the hospital and insisted on bringing him back to her home after the cast was put on. Marge told the county social services department that she was keeping Randy until he was healed. She didn't care what regulations or rules she broke about unauthorized visits.

For Randy it was like being a little boy again. He could call on his mother to wait on him, hand and foot. Marge fixed his favorite foods and carefully elevated his leg. She even gave him a sponge bath. But as the days wore on, Randy and Marge both saw the old tension come back. Randy pressed his mother to keep taking care of him like a little boy.

"Mom, you never got to do it before," Randy told his mother. "So you get to do it now."

After two weeks, Marge called Randy's social worker.

"He's ready to go back," she said.

Marge missed the next three planned visits and skipped our next review conference. I talked to Randy about what had happened. Randy seemed surprisingly content. He liked the care his mother gave him at her home when his ankle was fractured, but he wasn't surprised about her missing visits and meetings after she sent him back to his foster family.

"Could you talk to your mother while you were in her home?" I asked.

"Sometimes," Randy paused, "but it was hard to do it."

"I get scared, scared someone is going to take my life away," Randy continued later in our meeting. Randy again expressed a fear of hitting a wife or child. "When I get mad, I'm scared," he said. Randy said that he would berate himself about how "stupid" he was and then think to himself, "I want to take my own life."

"What helps?" I asked.

"I come to my senses....Wake up! I realize that this is a mistake." Randy said he would realize "somewhere in the mistake" was something he could learn to help him become "a better person."

"Yesterday I made a mistake, and today I look out for that mistake," he explained. We talked about how that changed his view of himself from "I am so stupid, I should be killed" to "I am so good. I get better every day. I learn from my mistakes."

Randy thought he was much more "free" at Sandy's home. He had been doing extremely well since returning from his mother's home. He even cleaned his room. Randy told me how he had earned an A for a gardening project at school. "I'm going to do some planting this spring at Sandy's house," Randy added.

"Somebody"

With the help of a broken ankle, Randy and Marge had tested whether they could live together again. Randy, who felt like he had lost his childhood as a boy, had a chance to be babied. He realized that Marge had tried again to be a mother to him—that she wanted the best for her son but could not raise him. They had both tried, and then by some unspoken mutual understanding, showed each other what they couldn't say out loud. Marge stayed away from Randy for the next three months, and he did not call her.

"I used to always do what my mind told me," Randy said. "Then I got into trouble." He realized that his mother had been trying to teach him lessons. "She was trying to make me a bigger person, teaching me, 'Don't let anyone push you over.' Now, I listen to my heart—my heart keeps me out trouble."

I invited Randy to imagine himself as a 27-year-old man with a strong heart. We did some imagery work with eye movements and Randy visualized his heart growing. He pictured a large red heart with four smaller hearts inside.

"What would help you become this 27-year-old?" I asked.

"I think of good things." Randy said he would "forget what other people say and keep smiling" if people teased him. If kids called him "stupid," he'd think of people who called him "smart and good."

"I would feel like somebody," said Randy.

The Cloud

Randy celebrated his 16th birthday at Sandy and Paul's home with their relatives. Marge sent a present but spoke to him only briefly on the phone.

Randy was doing well at school, in his horticulture program, and at Sandy and Paul's home, but he still worried about his temper taking over.

"Draw it for me," I asked.

Randy drew a giant black cloud shaped like an ice cream cone with five strokes of lightning blasting out like jagged swords.

"That's what I'm afraid of. If I'm with a girlfriend or my kids, well, I don't want to do to them like my mom did to me." Randy described how Marge had smacked him harder than even she was hit by his grandmother: "She hated me for who I am."

"Can you draw the opposite of the lightning and the cloud?" I asked.

Randy pictured a bright yellow sun. "I like to be a good guy—do the right thing."

As time went on, Randy continued to learn and thrive in Sandy and Paul's home. He tried out for the basketball team and started running distance races in track. By age 17, Randy described the hate inside him as much smaller than in his original picture. "Some people try to control other people when they're angry inside," Randy told me. "That's wrong. I don't want anybody controlling me. And, I know I can't get in control of myself by controlling other people. I used to do that."

Randy had stopped saying he wanted to kill himself when he felt stupid.

"Everyone would miss me," Randy said.

"Everyone" meant Sandy, Paul, their family, his mother, his child care worker, his social worker, and his teachers. When girls at school taunted him, he learned to firmly retort, "Don't scream at me." If he felt any impulses to hit a girl or a woman, Randy reminded himself quickly that that would be the end of him and "everyone would miss me." That kept him out of trouble.

"I'd miss me," he added with a smile.

Randy still had nightmares about his mother beating him, but he recognized that she had been using drugs that made her "bug out and not even know what she was doing." He said, "She told me she was wrong. She doesn't want me to do what she did." Finally, Randy was able to tell his mother what both of them already knew: "I'm not coming home."

Despite this breakthrough, Randy still struggled with the memories of his mother. A year without any fights ended abruptly when three girls in Randy's vocational training program called him racial slurs, kicked him hard when he wasn't looking, and called him "stupid."

"Don't scream at me.," Randy retorted. One of the girls charged up to Randy and slapped him on the face. Randy felt a pulsing, "like the blood flowing in my arms and then my body up into my head." He pushed the girl away, hard, and she fell backward on the floor. Randy stood over her, fists clenched.

The other girls screamed. A teacher rushed toward Randy and began talking to him, asking him to go to the office.

"I felt tired," Randy said of the fight. "I was wheezing, and I couldn't breathe...I couldn't get air. I thought I was going to die. I couldn't go into an office. I was afraid I'd smash the wall."

Randy just stood there frozen. The school called Sandy and asked her to take Randy home. The suspension note said he had hit a girl and refused to follow instructions.

"I let myself get out of control," Randy told me a few weeks later. "I thought, if they got frightened, maybe they'd think 'I shouldn't mess with him.'" Randy recognized that it didn't work out well. He had scared the teachers. "I'm going to get a friend, next time," he said. "She can go to the teachers. She can tell those girls to stop."

Randy's eyes had drifted off as he described not getting enough air. I knew he was remembering something else. "Did this ever happen before?" I asked.

"Once when I was 7, I couldn't breathe. My mom pushed a pillow on my face....she tried to suffocate me." Randy's face looked flushed as he spoke. "But all you have to do is bite the pillow. Bite a hole in it!" Randy quickly added. Randy believed he was to blame, as always, even for being suffocated.

Randy remembered practicing as a little boy how to hold his breath and try to control his heartbeat so he could go a long time without breathing. "I'd practice faking I was dead," he said. I asked Randy to visualize how big he was at age 7. What could he really have done? What would he expect a second grader to be able to do when a large adult was holding a pillow over his head?

I invited Randy to look at himself, now, as a 17-year-old, the size of a man. He was bigger than his mother. Several weeks later, with the help of his social worker, Randy told his mother that he would never hit any children he had, never strike them with a pot or a cord. Marge listened. Her eyes swelled and she looked like she was about to cry. Marge told Randy she was proud, proud he knew she was wrong to hit him, and proud he wouldn't hit his children.

Freedom

Randy beat the odds. But without Sandy and Paul, without the help of his social workers and child care workers, Randy very likely would have ended up incarcerated. Instead, at age 19, Randy was still doing well in Sandy and Paul's home.

"I see a big kid," Randy said about himself. Sandy and Paul allowed him time each day to act and feel like the 7-year-old boy he held deep inside. But Randy no longer got riled up when taunted. He didn't feel he had to stop every kid who threatened him.

"I'm the strong one," Randy told me. "I suffered the past. I survived."

My office phone rang. Randy's mother had arrived for our quarterly review conference. Randy beamed with delight. "I called her," he told me.

Randy escorted his mother up to my office. I watched them walk side by side. Randy now towered over his mother, and he matched her stride for stride. Marge smiled and looked at me. "He walks just like me," she said, then looked back at her son, smiling, as she met his eyes for just a second before Randy grinned and looked away.

In our meeting, Randy talked about how he'd like to teach other people about the lessons he learned. I thought to myself about what Randy had done. How many adults had the courage to go back to their parents and try again? How many adults have mustered the courage to talk to their parents about the wounds they carried inside from rejections and words said in anger? Randy had demonstrated the courage to discover the truth about his mother. Could she nurture and guide him now that both of them were older? Could she own what she had done? Randy had learned how to protect himself from the old nightmares, and all the while, he never killed the love he kept for his mother. Instead of drowning the old horrors in alcohol or drugs, or running away or fighting the world to forget the past, Randy grew taller, smarter, and braver.

Every time I met with Randy, I learned something new, something I could take home and use in my own life. The biggest lesson for me was about freedom.

America is built on the drive for freedom. We hear Patrick Henry's maxim, "Give me liberty or give me death," early in life. I learned from elementary school to admire heroes of the American Revolution, explorers who ventured into my home state of Michigan, and pioneers who settled the West. I was taught in story after story to value independence and autonomy, and to pass this on to my own children. By adolescence, my children, were bucking for drivers' licenses, absorbed in plans to go to college, and preparing to launch their own lives.

But Randy taught me a different lesson. "When I'm free, that's when I get into trouble," he said, his eyes cast downward. His chin rested on the large knuckles of his right hand, reminding me of Rodin's sculpture, *The Thinker*.

Randy had survived the worst rejection, the experience of his mother wanting to end his life out of her own pain, exasperation, and drug-induced rage. He knew firsthand the cost of adults running from their pain. Randy had lived with his mother's addiction, her isolation, and her depression.

At 19, Randy had been advised by the New York State Department of Social Services that he could go off on his own and lead his own life. He no longer had to be monitored by a county social services worker. Randy was a legal adult, free to leave the system. He could move into an apartment subsidized by public assistance while he looked for a job or continued to go to school. Randy could get away from adults telling him what to do. Freedom was at hand.

"I'm staying with Sandy and Paul," Randy told me. I thought of what Randy was teaching me. Unlike so many youth his age, Randy knew what he needed to *really* be free. Randy realized that freedom meant feeling strong and safe enough to be honest with the people you love, to be able to face the truth, without living every day dreading another beating or being cast out alone. Freedom meant having people who could love you for being 19 on the outside and 7 within. Randy knew how much he needed Sandy and Paul, their home, and their family.

The Crystal Ball

Randy smiled, a wide grin spreading from cheek to cheek. His eyes sparkled. It was the week after Thanksgiving. "I am in the present. I am in my own future now," he told me.

Sandy and Paul, Randy's foster parents, had invited Marge, Randy's mother, to join them for Thanksgiving. Randy had agreed to the invitation but didn't think his mother would really come. Part of him didn't want her to come. Why take a chance on ruining the holiday?

Sandy and Randy got up early that morning and drove an hour to pick up Marge at her apartment. Marge brought one of her favorite pies. Randy baked cookies and cakes. Sandy and her older children prepared the turkey, potatoes, and vegetables. Two families, together, sharing the holiday.

"It was good," Randy smiled, remembering the dinner as we talked in my office.

"How did you get along with your mom?" I asked.

"Well," Randy smiled again. "There's the Mom who took care of me. There's the Mom who hit me."

"What's different now?"

"I used to live in the badness. Some people go through a lot of badness. I had more than lots of people. Everybody has a black hole inside them."

"What would the badness look like, if you put it into one shape?" I asked, handing Randy some paper and markers.

Randy sketched a crystal ball with dark wavering lines inside.

"How does it work?" I asked.

"I wish I could just reach inside and take the bad feelings out. I'd just let them go. I just want to free myself." Randy paused, his eyes cast downward, his chin resting on the knuckles of his right hand. "But when I'm free, that's when I get in trouble."

"What could you do with the bad feelings? So you could keep them safe?" I asked.

Randy added a keyhole in the base of the crystal ball.

"It's locked. I've got the key," he said.

"I used to wish I was invisible," Randy added, his smile gone, and his eyes looking upward. Small furrows creased his forehead. "I know no one is perfect," he said. He tightened his jaw. "But this is *my* life."

PART III

Healing Our Children, Healing Ourselves

15

MOLLIE

*The moral universe rests upon
the breath of schoolchildren.*

–Rabbi Yehuda Nisiah, cir. 250 B.C.E.
Cited by Vivian Paley in The Kindness of Children

A chunky-cheeked little cherub, Mollie had lived five of her six years with neglect and violence before CPS removed her from her home. After her parents surrendered her for adoption, Mollie often cried at night, upset that her parents had not come back to see her on her birthday or Christmas, as they had promised.

I asked Mollie what she looked for in a mother and father.

"Mothers should cook food, buy snacks, give hugs and kisses, give me rewards, keep me safe, and be there."

"What about fathers?" I asked.

"Fathers should be good, love children, be good to children, make them happy, do not hurt me, keep me safe, and cook food."

"And what should girls and boys do?" I asked.

"Girls need to do their homework, not lie, not steal, be good," Mollie replied.

"So simple," I thought to myself, and yet, I knew that Mollie had never had parents like this. But that didn't stop her from continuing to search. Mollie wanted parents who could help her to understand what had happened in her life.

I found myself smiling at Mollie. I was inspired by her determination to keep looking for moms and dads who cared enough to parent a hurt child. Mollie's tenacity and faith helped keep my own hope alive for children like her—and for all of us.

16

Nurturing the Angels in Our Lives

Insight is wrestled from adversity.

–Rabbi Steven Leder
The Extraordinary Nature of Ordinary Things

*M*y agency's executive director once compared child and family services to MASH units in an unending war. Like physicians on the front lines, my colleagues and I work with shortages and extreme risk. It often seems like we are being battered with cutbacks, regulations, and audits by the governmental bodies that should be our allies. Like many practitioners, I was drawn to child and family services to help and to heal, and I have experienced how my colleagues and I sometimes become overwhelmed by the magnitude of families' crises compared to the meager resources available to help.

In the United States, we pay our parking attendants more to watch our cars than we pay the professionals responsible for the safety and education of troubled children. Tollbooth operators often earn more than social workers grappling with domestic violence, sexual abuse, and suicidal behavior. I get discouraged when I see adept, caring practitioners leave child and family services to find less stressful, better paid jobs.

The emotional cost has been high for me, as well. I have often come home feeling weary and irritable after hearing young adults tell me of rapes and beatings, seeing the tears on a young mother's face, feeling the frenzy of a terrified child, or watching siblings shuffle between foster homes with their belongings stuffed into black plastic bags. Caring for these families means feeling the pain and danger in their lives. Taking on too much pain can leave practitioners exhausted and burned out, but blocking out the pain means we're not emotionally available to either our clients or our families and friends. At points, I have taken refuge in cynicism or distanced myself emotionally, pulling away from colleagues and even my own family. I have thought about leaving this work.

But working in child and family services also means experiencing again and again the rekindling of hope—and reigniting a passion for living. In its own way, it is addictive. The rewards come in small but meaningful changes in a child's trust and a parent's commitment. These changes may begin with a child's tears and a parent's outstretched arms breaking through years of silence and anger, the smile on a child's face as he goes home after weeks or months in placement, or the calm look from a parent as she sets a limit for a previously out-of-control youth. When parents and other caring adults reconnect to a child, you can almost feel an electric current linking their shared smiles, tears, and each embrace. Parents become empowered with new vigor. Children who entered placement after hurting themselves or someone else return home from placement or move into adoptive families with renewed hope and go on to become honor roll students and graduate from high school to the delight of their families and friends.

Though many of them lived for years with terrible violence, abuse, and neglect, the children who cried to me were not tragedies. Each of them showed me a strong drive to rebuild their families and the energy to make their needs known. Like angels, they shone a beacon on the unspoken dangers and unresolved heartbreak in their families. They fought with all their strength for ways to reunite their families and forge a new future.

Children in crisis tell us what has happened before and warn us of what will happen again if their family's pain remains buried. They push us to see what is missing and what needs to change. But children can't make these changes happen alone. The adults in their lives have the power to alter the way a child experiences the world, or to let a child's hope wither and die. Likewise, professionals can choose to coax out the caring part of a child at risk, or we can ignore the child's message and focus instead on the negative behaviors through which the child's message manifests itself. But when parents, authorities, or practitioners only seek to temporarily contain an out-of-control youth by force, with penalties, walls, or guards, we leave the nightmare intact. The unspoken pain simmers and burns—and eventually explodes.

I have learned that children cannot wait months and years for their parents or other adults to take responsibility. Nor can communities: The damage is too great and the risk is too high. The choices we make now determine the difference between another generation of trauma and children leading a better life. I also know that the caring that my colleagues, my neighbors, and I show for children at risk will determine our own quality of life and that of our children: The children we serve today will someday be our neighbors in our communities, for better or for worse.

I know, too, that children in acute crisis show us in stark terms what we *all* need to survive and to succeed. If we dare to look deep inside ourselves, the voices and behaviors of troubled children can be seen as reflections of our shared need to heal our own families and overcome our own traumas. Looking back now, I recognize how I have grappled with my own inner angel, the cries from deep inside me that called out for resolution.

We find the angel inside every child by listening to the feelings they stir within us, the fears, the anger, the despair, and the yearning to be valued and loved. To recognize wounded children means acknowledging our own vulnerability. At the same time, by listening to what children are teaching us, we can become stronger than our fears.

By answering a child's call for help, we become the real-life heroes children need to become whole again, the angels in their lives—and in our own. In this way, each child's story becomes our story. And helping a troubled child rewrite the story of his or her life restores hope for all of us.

Resources for Caring Adults

Angels and the Search for Meaning

Cohen, N. J. (1995). *Self, struggle and change: Family conflict stories in Genesis and their healing insights for our lives.* Woodstock, VT: Jewish Lights.

Freeman, E. F. (1994). *Angelic healing.* New York: Warner.

Godwin, M. (1990). *Angels: An endangered species.* New York: Simon and Schuster.

Kedar, K. (1999). *God whispers: Stories of the soul, lessons of the heart.* Woodstock, VT: Jewish Lights.

Kushner, L. (1994). *God was in this place & I did not know it.* Woodstock, VT: Jewish Lights.

Kushner, L. (1996). *Invisible lines of connection: Sacred stories of the ordinary.* Woodstock, VT: Jewish Lights.

Lewis, J. R., & Oliver, E. D. (1996). *Angels A to Z.* New York: Gale Research.

Margolies, M. (1994). *A gathering of angels.* New York: Ballantine.

Rosenbloom, S. (1998, Summer). Finding blessing in being a Jewish man today: Limping Jacob's limp. *Brotherhood Magazine.*

Attachment Research and Interventions

Ainsworth, M. D. S., Blehar, M. C., Waters, B., & Wall, S. (1978). *Patterns of attachment: A psychological study of the strange situation.* Hillsdale, NJ: Lawrence Erlbaum.

Beringen, Z. (1994). Attachment theory and research: Application to clinical practice. *American Journal of Orthopsychiatry, 6,* 404–420.

Bowlby, J. (1988). *A secure base: Parent-child attachment and healthy human development.* New York: Basic Books.

Delaney, R. (1997). *Healing power.* Oklahoma City, OK: Woods 'N' Barnes.

167

Delaney, R. (1998a). *Fostering changes.* Oklahoma City, OK: Woods 'N' Barnes.

Delaney, R. (1998b). *Raising Cain.* Oklahoma City, OK: Woods 'N' Barnes.

Hughes, D. (1997). *Facilitating developmental attachment.* Northvale, NJ: Jason Aronson.

Hughes, D. (1998). *Building the bonds of attachment: Awakening love in deeply troubled children.* Northvale, NJ: Jason Aronson.

James, B. (1994). *Handbook for treatment of attachment-trauma problems in children.* New York: Lexington.

Kagan, R. (in press). *Rebuilding attachments with traumatized children: Healing from losses, violence, abuse, and neglect.* Binghamton, NY: Haworth Press.

Levy, T., & Orlans, M. (1998). *Attachment, trauma, and healing: Understanding and treating attachment disorder in children and families.* Washington, DC: CWLA Press.

Mahler, M., Pine, F., & Bergman, A. (1975). *The psychological birth of the human infant.* New York: Basic Books.

Pastzor, E. M., Leighton, M., & Blome, W. W. (1993). *Helping children and youths develop positive attachments.* Washington, DC: CWLA Press.

Peterson, J. (1994). *The invisible road: Parental insights to attachment disorder.* (Available from author).

Schore, A. (1994) *Affect regulation and the origin of the self: The neurobiology of emotional development.* Hillsdale, NJ: Lawrence Erlbaum.

Schore, A. N. (2001). The effects of early relational trauma on right brain development, affect regulation, and infant mental health. *Infant Mental Health Journal, 22,* 201–269.

Siegel, D. (1999). *The developing mind.* New York: Guilford Press.

Child and Family Services / At-Risk Youth

Brendtro, L. K., Brokenleg, M., & Van Bockean, S. (1990). *Reclaiming youth at risk: Our hope for the future.* Bloomington, IN: National Education Service.

Brooks, R. (1991). *The self-esteem teacher.* Circle Pines, MN: American Guidance Service.

Brooks, R. (1994). Children at risk: Fostering resilience and hope. *American Journal of Orthopsychiatry, 64,* 545–553.

Bronfenbrenner, U. (1979). *The ecology of human development.* Cambridge, MA: Harvard University Press.

Cavanagh Johnson, T. (1998). *Treatment exercises for child abuse victims and children with sexual behavior problems.* (Available from author: 1101 Fremont Ave., Suite 101, South Pasadena, CA 91030).

Edelman, M. (1992). *A measure of our success.* Boston: Beacon Press.

Eron, L. D., Gentry, J. H., & Schlegel, P. (1994). *Reason to hope: A psychosocial perspective on violence & youth.* Washington, DC: American Psychological Association.

Eggert, L. L. (1994). *Anger management for youth: Stemming aggression and violence.* Bloomington, IN: National Educational Service.

Fahlberg, V. (1991). *A child's journey through placement.* Indianapolis, IN: Perspectives Press.

Finkelstein, N. E. (1991). *Children and youth in limbo: A search for connections.* New York: Praeger.

Garbarino, J. (1995). *Raising children in a socially toxic environment.* San Francisco: Jossey-Bass.

Garbarino, J. (1999). *Lost boys: Why our sons turn violent and how we can save them.* New York: Free Press.

Gelles, R. (1997). *Intimate violence in families* (3rd ed.). Thousand Oaks, CA: Sage.

Gil, E. (1986). *A book for kids who were abused.* San Francisco: Launch Press.

Gil, E. (1988). *Treatment of adult survivors of childhood abuse.* Walnut Creek, CA: Launch Press.

Gil, E. (1991). *The healing power of play.* New York: Guilford.

Gil, E. (1996). *Treating abused adolescents.* New York: Guilford.

Gurian, M. (1997). *The wonder of boys.* New York: J. P. Tarcher.

Gurian, M. (1999). *A fine young man: What parents, mentors, and educators can do to shape adolescent boys into exceptional men.* New York: J. P. Tarcher.

Kagan, R., & Schlosberg, S. (1989). *Families in perpetual crisis.* New York: Norton.

Kagan, R. (1996). *Turmoil to turning points: Building hope for children in crisis placements.* New York: Norton.

Kaplan, L., & Girard, J. L. (1994). *Strengthening high-risk families: A handbook for practitioners.* New York: Lexington Books.

Klass, C. S. (1996). *Home visiting.* Baltimore: Brookes.

Kindlon, D. J., Thompson, M., et al. (1999). *Raising Cain: Protecting the emotional life of boys.* New York: Ballantine.

Larson, S., & Brendtro, L. (2000). *Reclaiming our prodigal sons and daughters: A practical approach for connecting with youth in conflict.* Bloomington, IN: National Education Service.

Linesch, D. (1993). *Art therapy with families in crisis: Overcoming resistance through non-verbal expression.* New York: Brunner/Mazel.

Munson, L., & Riskin, K. (1995). *In their own words: A sexual abuse workbook for teenage girls.* Washington, DC: Child Welfare League of America.

Nadeau, K. G., & Dixon, E. B. (1997). *Learning to slow down and pay attention: A book for kids about ADD.* Washington, DC: Magination Press.

Pipher, M. (1994). *Saving Ophelia: Saving the selves of adolescent girls.* New York: Ballantine.

Pipher, M. (1996). *The shelter of each other.* New York: Putnam.

Pollack, W. S. (1998). *Real boys: Rescuing our sons from the myths of boyhood.* New York: Random House.

Schorr, L. B. (1998). *Common purpose: Strengthening families and neighborhoods to rebuild America.* Doubleday / Anchor.

Steinhauer, P. (1991). *The least detrimental alternative: A systematic guide to case planning and decision making for children in care.* Toronto, Canada: University of Toronto Press.

Straus, M. A. (1994). *Beating the devil out of them.* New York: Lexington Books.

Straus, M. (1999). *No-talk therapy for children and adolescents.* New York: Norton.

van Gulden, H., & Bartels-Rabb, L. M. (1995). *Real parents, real children: Parenting the adopted child.* New York: Crossroads.

Way, N. (1998). *Everyday courage: The lives and stories of urban teenagers.* New York: University Press.

Parenting and Healthy Development

Brazelton, T. (1974). *Touchpoints.* Boulder, CO: Perseus Press.

Brazelton, T. & Cramer, B. G. (1990). *The earliest relationship.* New York: Addison-Wesley.

Butterfield, P., et al. (1997). *Play and learning.* Denver, CO: How to Read Your Baby, Inc.

Butterfield, P., et al. (1997). *Love is layers of sharing.* Denver, CO: How to Read Your Baby, Inc.

Dodson, F. (1992). *How to father.* Seattle, WA: Signet.

Dodson, F. (1992). *How to parent.* New York: New American Library.

Lansky, V. (1993). *Games babies play.* Deephaven, MN: Book Peddlers.

Manolson, A. (1995). *You can make the difference.* Toronto, Canada: Hanen Centre.

Morin, V. (1993). *Messy activities and more.* Chicago: Chicago Review Press.

Small, M. (1998). *Our babies, ourselves: How biology and culture shape the way we parent.* New York: Anchor Books.

Zero To Three. (1997). *How I grow in your care from zero to three.* Arlington, VA: National Center for Infants, Toddlers, and Families.

Psychotherapeutic Approaches for Trauma

Calof, D. L. (1996). *The couple who became each other and other tales from a hypnotherapist's casebook.* New York: Bantam.

Figley, C. (1989). *Helping traumatized families.* San Francisco: Jossey-Bass.

Gil, E. (1991). *The healing power of play.* New York: Guilford.

Gil, E. (1996). *Treating abused adolescents.* New York: Guilford.

James, B. (1989). *Treating traumatized children.* Lexington, MA: Lexington Books.

Nichols, M. (1995). *Facing shame so we can find self-respect.* Amherst, NY: Prometheus Books.

Shapiro, F. (1995). *Eye movement desensitization and reprocessing.* New York: Guilford.

Shapiro, F., & Forrest, M. S. (1997). *EMDR: The breakthrough therapy for overcoming anxiety, stress, and trauma.* New York: Basic Books.

Terr, L. (1990). *Too scared to cry.* New York: Harper and Row.

Tinker, R. H., & Wilson, S. A. (1999) *Through the eyes of a child: EMDR with children.* New York: Norton.

van der Kolk, B. A. (2001). The assessment and treatment of complex PTSD. In R. Yehuda (Ed.), *Traumatic stress.* Arlington, VA: American Psychiatric Press.

van der Kolk, B. A., McFarlane, A. C., & Weisaeth, L. (Eds.) (1996). *Traumatic stress.* New York: Guilford.

Storytelling and Narrative Therapies

Bettelheim, B. (1975). *The uses of enchantment: The meaning and importance of fairy tales.* New York: Vintage Books.

Combs, G., & Freedman, J. (1990). *Symbol, story, and ceremony: Using metaphor in individual and family therapy.* New York: Norton.

Duhl, B. (1983). *From the inside out and other metaphors.* New York: Brunner/Mazel.

Evans, M. D. (1986). *This is me and my two families.* New York: Magination Press.

Freedman, J., & Combs, G. (1996). *Narrative therapy: The social construction of preferred realities.* New York: Norton.

Gardner, R. (1975). *Psychotherapeutic approaches to the resistant child.* New York: Jason Aronson.

Gardner, R. (1986). *Therapeutic communication with children.* New Jersey: Jason Aronson.

Grinder, J., & Bandler, R. (1976). *The structure of magic.* CA: Science and Behavior Books.

Jewett, C. (1978). *Adopting the older child.* Cambridge, MA: Harvard Common Press.

Kagan, R. (1982). Storytelling and game therapy for children in placement. *Child*

Care Quarterly, II, 280–290.

Kagan, R. (in press). *Real life heroes: A life storybook for children.* Binghamton, NY: Haworth Press.

Kagan, R. (2000)."My game": Rebuilding hope for children in placement. In C. E. Schaefer & S. E. Reid (Eds.), *Game play: Therapeutic uses of childhood games.* New York: Wiley.

Lankton, C., & Lankton, S. (1989). *Tales of enchantment.* New York: Brunner/ Mazel.

Munson, L., & Riskin, K. (1995). *In their own words: A sexual abuse workbook for teenage girls.* Washington, DC: Child Welfare League of America.

Paley, V. (1999). *The kindness of children.* Cambridge, MA: Harvard University Press.

Roberts, J. (1994). *Tales and transformations—Stories in families and family therapy.* New York: Norton.

Suddaby, K., & Landau, J. (1998). Positive and negative timelines: A technique for restorying. *Family Process, 37,* 287–297.

Wheeler, C. (1978). *Where am I going? Making a child's life story book.* Juneau, AK: Winking Owl Press.

White, M., & Epston, D. (1990). *Narrative means to therapeutic ends.* New York: Norton.

Whitehouse, E., & Pudney, W. (1996). *A volcano in my tummy.* Gabriola Island, Canada: New Society.

Child and Family Organizations

American Bar Association Center on Children and the Law
740 15th Street, NW
Washington, DC 20005
202/662-1720
www.abanet.org/child

Annie E. Casey Foundation Family to Family Reconstructing Foster Care Initiative
410/547-6600
800/222-1099
www.aecf.org/initiatives/familytofamily/

American Humane Association, Children's Division
63 Inverness Drive East
Englewood, CO 80112
866/242-1877
www.americanhumane.org

Center for the Study and Prevention of Violence
  University of Colorado Campus Box 442
  Boulder, CO 80309
  303/492-8465
  www.colorado.edu/cspv/

"Just for Kids!" Program Family Life Development Center
  Cornell University
  Martha Van Rensselaer Hall
  Ithaca, NY 14853-4401
  607/255-7794
  www.research.cornell.edu/vpr/CenterDir/famlife.html

Children's Defense Fund
  25 E Street, NW
  Washington, DC 20001
  800/CDF-1200
  www.childrensdefense.org

Child Welfare League of America
  440 First Street NW. Third Floor
  Washington DC 20001-2085
  202/638-2952
  www.cwla.org

Fight Crime: Invest in Kids
  1334 G Street, NW, Suite B
  Washington, DC 20005-3107
  202/898-0792
  www.fightcrime.org

Healthy Families America (Prevent Child Abuse America)
  200 S. Michigan Avenue, 17th Floor
  Chicago, IL 60604-2404
  312/663-3520
  www.healthyfamiliesamerica.org

National Association for the Education of Young Children
  1509 16th Street, NW
  Washington DC 20036
  www.naeyc.org

National Center on Child Abuse Prevention Research (Prevent Child Abuse
  America)
  200 S. Michigan Avenue, 17th Floor
  Chicago, IL 60604-2404
  312/663-3520
  www.preventchildabuse.org/learn_more/research.html

National Child Traumatic Stress Initiative, Program Office
    Center for Mental Health Services
    Substance Abuse and Mental Health Services Administration
    Department of Health and Human Services
    5600 Fishers Lane
    Parklawn Building, Room 17C - 26
    Rockville, MD 20857
    301/443-2940

The National Court Appointed Special Advocate Association (CASA)
    100 West Street, North Tower, Suite500
    Seattle, WA 98119
    800/628-5238
    www.nationalcasa.org

The National Foster Parent Association
    P.O. Box 81
    Alpha, OH 45301
    800/557-5238
    www.nfpainc.org

Parents as Teachers National Center
    10176 Corporate Square Drive, Suite 230
    St. Louis, MO 63132
    314/432-4330
    www.patnc.org

ABOUT THE AUTHOR

*R*ichard Kagan, PhD, has 26 years of postdoctoral experience in child and family, mental health, and substance abuse services as a therapist, consultant, trainer, researcher, and director of psychological services, research, and professional development programs. He is the author and coauthor of five books about child and family services: *Families in Perpetual Crisis* with Shirley Schlosberg; *Turmoil to Turning Points: Building Hope for Children in Crisis Placements; Rebuilding Attachments with Traumatized Children: Healing from Losses, Violence, Abuse, and Neglect; Real Life Heroes: A Life Storybook for Children;* and *Wounded Angels: Lessons of Courage from Children in Crisis.* Dr. Kagan has also published more than 20 articles, chapters, and papers on practice and research issues in family systems work, child welfare, adoption, professional development, program evaluation, and quality improvement in family service agencies. Professional honors include two awards for distinguished achievement in child and family services. He has been a workshop leader and keynote speaker at national and international conferences of family therapy, psychology, and child welfare associations in the United States, Europe, and Asia; at annual conferences sponsored by family service agencies in the United States and Canada; and at state conferences of home-based family service associations. Currently, he is Director of Psychological Services at Parsons Child and Family Center in Albany, New York, and Clinical Director/ Principal Investigator for Parsons Child Trauma Study Center, a community services site for the National Child Traumatic Stress Network.